'LOVED *The Alchemy*: it's wha
writer needs; a friend who is at t
but also kind, funny, compass
what it's like to feel insecure, but who has been through ...,
kind of fire, and has come out indestructible.'

Joanne Harris

'This beautiful and empathetic book seeks to recover for writers the immense value of what Wordsworth calls "wise passiveness" that "can feed this mind of ours". It reminds us that not-writing is sometimes a kind of writing, and of the importance of downtime, productive failure and bubble baths. Anna Vaught's unique writing guide is, above all, an act of kindness to authors everywhere.'

Jonathon Taylor, author and Professor of Creative Writing,
University of Leicester

'*The Alchemy* is the writing guide we all need: wise, funny, deeply compassionate, it meets us where we are and gently suggests that's a place where wonderful things can happen. Do not despair – read this instead.'

Shelley Harris, author, lecturer in English Literature and Director
of MA Creative Writing Programme, University of Reading

'I was completely blown away by *The Alchemy*. Anna Vaught will liberate you from the trappings of perfection and teach you how to create incredible things from every single piece of you, including all those bits you believed were always holding you back. This is not just for writers: I think *everyone* should read this book.'

Kat Ashton, Head of Courses, Jericho Writers

The
Alchemy

a guide to gentle productivity

for writers

ANNA VAUGHT

HAY PRESS

HAY PRESS
10 High Town
Hay-on-Wye
HR3 5AE

an imprint of

RENARD PRESS LTD
124 City Road, London EC1V 2NX
United Kingdom

info@renardpress.com
020 8050 2928
www.haypress.co.uk

The Alchemy first published by Hay Press in 2023

Text © Anna Vaught, 2023
Foreword © Chris Laoutaris, 2023

Cover design and illustrations by Will Dady

Printed in the United Kingdom by Severn

ISBN: 978-1-80447-040-4

9 8 7 6 5 4 3 2 1

Quotations from third parties are reproduced with their kind permission. Every effort has been made to ascertain the copyright status of quoted works, but if any oversight has been made we will be happy to make corrections in future editions.

CLIMATE POSITIVE Renard Press is proud to be a climate positive publisher, removing more carbon from the air than we emit and planting a small forest. For more information see renardpress.com/eco.

Contents

First of all, do not skip this bit. *You skipped this bit, didn't you?* If you didn't, here is what you will find in this book, with a little information on its structure and how to use it.

The Alchemy
In each chapter there will be a brief tip on gentle productivity provided by writers I admire and adore. You will discover that there are essays, too, because I could not show you this book without showing you who and what I was; am. There are some rude words here and there, and I hope that is all right. Good, I'm glad you don't mind, because I have always distrusted people who don't curse. After most chapters there is a writing exercise.

Foreword

I was hard-wired to feel like a failure, scared of exposure and I did not have a voice.

Anna Vaught's *The Alchemy* is the indispensable guide for anyone who is a writer, is struggling to write, or wants to write. Compassionate, patient and liberatingly honest, Vaught takes you by the hand and shows you how life's obstacles, struggles and traumas are the gateways to creative possibilities, to new 'ways of seeing' and new ways of writing. She gives you the tools to free your voice, to reimagine what writing is, and what it can be. This book unlocks the magic in a chance encounter in a supermarket, in a path walked or a road not taken, in the wisdom born from suffering, in a daily routine and even in the abyss of despair, because at 'the heart of sadness is a miracle' too, waiting to be transmuted into text. Radically irreverent, it takes a sledgehammer to the tyranny of concepts like failure and perfection, weaponises self-doubt, fear and rage, and empowers you to embrace the uniqueness of your own expression. *The Alchemy* is a manifesto for the dispossessed, marginalised, burdened, tired and weird

– because 'weird is great' – and it will help you 'find your weird' and turn it into gold. To read this marvellous and life-changing book is to open up glittering horizons you have been told you should not dare to dream; to unleash the rebel-writer in you. Add it to your arsenal and be part of the insurrection!

Dr Chris Laoutaris

Associate Professor
The Shakespeare Institute, University of Birmingham,
and author of *Shakespeare's Book*

The
Alchemy

A short companion to your writing life: a practical guide to gentle productivity by one who knows and had little time or energy.

For Elijah.
You are the alchemy and you, above all,
helped make this book.

'Nature, one lights you up with his ardour,
Another puts you in mourning.
What says "Burial" to one
Says to another: "Life and splendour"!'
'The Alchemy of Sorrow',
Charles Baudelaire[1]

Alchemy: The medieval forerunner of chemistry, focusing on the transmutation of matter – particularly attempting to convert base metals into gold and find a universal elixir.
Late Middle English via Old French and medieval Latin from Arabic al-kīmiyā', from al (the) + kīmiyā' (from Greek khēmia, 'art of transmuting metals').

Or, to put it another way, any magical power or process of transmuting a common substance, usually of little value, into a substance of great value.

---

1 Charles Baudelaire, 'The Alchemy of Sorrow' (*'Alchimie de la douleur'*), from *Les Fleurs du Mal* (1857).

Welcome

The Alchemy is about writing a book – a work of fiction of whatever kind – when you thought you could not. This is a book for everyone, but with a particular eye on those who are tired and lacking in confidence; those who are disabled, chronically ill or perhaps care for a loved one who would struggle without them. Essentially, this has been me for some time now, and that is how I know about productivity – and how I know about challenging what it is; how we think of and understand productivity in terms of a creative project.

I thrived not only from deadlines, spreadsheets and flow charts (although these things are excellent), but from learning to work with what I had, when I could and, also, in understanding that writing a book happens all the time. Much of what can become a book, or deepen what you already have, might be found in being observant in your daily life – insofar as you can be, because I want to exclude no one here. Not everyone will be active.

I want to free you from the idea that you must write every day to be a writer, or even if you want to complete a full-length book. If that works for you, wonderful, but it won't work for everyone, and won't be possible for many. So I try to get us to think about the creation of a book in different terms: in observations, but also in knowing that thinking is also a huge part of the job. Give yourself unhurried time in which to do this.

In laying all this out, I am going to offer you various essays full of ideas and first-hand experiences, and I will suggest writing exercises as I go. Finally, I am going to offer thoughts on sending out work and navigating the industry, looking after your mental health as you go.

This is a book for beginners, but it might also be for you if you are stuck in your habits and practice; perhaps you are newly unwell or constrained in some way, or perhaps you just need a pal to guide you through the day-to-day with the book you want to write.

As we go, I will also say a few things about the industry as I have experienced it or as it has been experienced by others who have generously shared their experience with me, or others who would rather not have shared their experience, but felt compelled to because they were not coping. That happens, too. If it does, you need to know that you are not alone, because feeling like you *are* is devastating. A wise and frankly bestselling and absolutely no-shit author shared this with me when I nearly gave up.

A final word: I am a Celt and I bear a grudge, so just to say that if you were ever unpleasant in a sustained way, tried your gaslight on or radically thwarted me, I have most likely parodied you in this book and put it in my special ledger: *THE BIG BOOK OF CELTIC GRUDGES*.

*Oh – and a little something to remember. Thinking of productivity in terms of writing on a page, if you only wrote a hundred words a day, then in two years you would have a novel. Not publishable words, but ready for edits, assuming you edit at the end like I do (caveat: test it on your pulse and try it out; do what feels right for you, though, which might be to edit as you go).

What does 100 words look like on a page? From one asterisk to another (look back, reader). *Here* are your one hundred words!*

Remember this, too: 'A journey of a thousand miles must begin with the first step' wrote (probably) Lao Tzu in the *Tao Te Ching* in about 400 BC, and I am sure he would be delighted to discover how many fridge magnets and inspirational quotation posters he is on today. However, it is true. Keep moving forward.

Also, a novel (for example) of 50,000 words or more starts with the hundred words which you wrote in bed, and maybe while you were crying and howling into your void of waning self-belief. *I* said that in 2023 – only, it's no good for a fridge magnet or any other merchandise as it's not succinct. One more thing: making a novel does not come with a one-size-fits-all set of instructions. So please alter anything you need, as you go, and trust yourself to do this. That, in itself, is a vital step.

So, welcome to *The Alchemy*. As I said, it is about authoring a book – a work of fiction of whatever kind – when you thought you could not. It is about learning to work with what you have – a sort of alchemy, turning base metals into gold – when you can, and discovering that writing your book happens all the time.

Let us begin.

Just a warning – a trigger warning. For this book to be as authentic as possible I am frank, but be aware that mental health and childhood trauma are referred to. Also, if you were reading the list of contents, I swear a bit. You will also find there is some overlap between chapters and that I reiterate some points. It's intended as a refrain and to be of comfort to you – a bit of surreptitious learning by rote, and is not there because I wasn't edited, I promise.

Introduction

Who Am I and Who Are You?

More about the book, how you might use it and its ideas.

I took a long time to be published. By that I mean I took a long time *to start writing*. I did not have the confidence. Now I have, it is like a torrent. I am seven years in. When the occasional person decides to be a bit snarky about the fact I have written nine books − one in translation with which I was fully involved, a proposal on submission and two more which were terrible and thus I carved them up and developed them into short fiction pieces, in that time also writing two major columns, inaugurating a literary prize and writing fifty seven reviews, stories and features − I tend to explain that they were in my head for decades and that's why everything is as it is now. *My bravehearts, do your own thing; believe in your work first and foremost, and do not apologise for the way in which you work, whether it be 'too fast' or 'too slow'.* Here is my first bit of love for you all, and it is about productivity − but perhaps not in the way you might expect. It is also about being gentle on yourself and always working with what you have.

There is more. I am not one to blow my own trumpet, and frankly even writing this makes me feel (apologies) that I might throw up on my own feet. *Eugh.* It is uncomfortable for me, BUT HERE WE ARE ANYWAY. I have written a great deal in seven years, and what you are reading is my eighth published book. Partly because of stress and sadness, I had a huge fuck-it moment and started writing a book. I had put this off for decades because I was sure that writing was for other people. You know the other people. Fancy people. People who have it all together. Those things which you suspect are not true of you. Fancy things, sophisticated things, writery (that can be a word for the purposes of *The Alchemy*) things. I had been raised to think poorly of myself and, in a moment of rage which bubbled up, I thought F*** IT, and also, F*** YOU. I started then and there and kept going until I had a book. A horrible, messy first draft. At last I had a start, and have not stopped since. I am aware I work quickly: that is not a special skill, but just the velocity which is natural to me; it is not a target. I have, however, used all the strategies we will unfold together in this book, learning them more deeply and powerfully as I went.

It is magic, you know, but I understand that putting a book together starts with a leap of faith and, depending on what you have ingested, primarily about yourself and who you are, it can be a challenging thing. I am with you, though, through this book.

I asked others about not pursuing writing when they wanted to, and here are some telling responses. I bet they are familiar to you, too, which is why I wanted to include them, in composite. I was told about self-sabotage, procrastination. Highly likely undiagnosed

ADHD. Self-esteem issues. Breadwinner – people could not afford to stop work and work takes up too much brainpower and executive function. I also saw extraordinary lack of confidence where writers stated that they did not know they had got anything done or how they managed to complete an MFA: it must have been a fluke. I heard how self-esteem, lack of self-belief, the pressure from family to get a "proper" job stopped people from even starting. There is, of course, taking a leap of faith, but it is not only that: structural inequality is real, and lack of opportunity is real. I hope that this book helps to give us all tools.

So let's go on this adventure together. For a start, *you work with what you have.* That is, it's lovely to have an office or a dedicated room, but if circumstances demand that you write at your kitchen table, or on your lap wherever you are, so be it. If you wait for those perfect circumstances, you will never start, so yes: always go with what you have. I write at the kitchen table and am frequently interrupted. I go with it and use headphones for busy times. Remember that genius exists in the finest library, but also at a scruffy kitchen table. Also, if you think you must assemble ideal conditions – that is, ideal emotional or psychological conditions – before you write or continue writing, then I do believe that is deferring your creativity to fate. You may feel down, sad or that heavy weight of grief that comes after the first pains which you think will kill you. My darlings, I am so, so sorry. But you know, you can write in rage and sadness, too. Maybe not yet, but you will. Sometimes, little bits of story unfurl within the sad story of you and yours; cling to them, because they are still there, and they are precious. Think I don't know? I am writing this now, to you after a second very broken night,

11

and this little story unfurled while I was on the phone to care providers and emergency staff because I have a very unwell eldest. I find it heartbreaking sometimes, and after years it seems a solution is not within our grasp; but within those feelings, I try to draw something else out. Today, this morning, I was so tired, *it was for you. Take it.*

It may seem, when we or those we care for face difficulties in our daily life, that we cannot create, *but that is not so*. Here is more about me: I manage long-standing mental-health problems and I have been recovering from Long Covid (we are getting to know each a bit better, right?) – and I am not writing from a position of privilege, telling you sweet things. I am aiming to comfort you, so that you might follow a dream – *your dream of writing a book* – something so many of us aspire to, and, hopefully, get paid for it, too – but we will come back to the latter.

What about the adage of writing every day? That *real* writers write every day. Well, lovely if this is you, but it cannot be everyone. I cannot do it. If you are poorly or managing any combination of circumstances – or even if it is just a case that this does not work for you – then you cannot do it. This does not mean you cannot produce a book. Again, go with what is available to you because, and I cannot emphasise this enough, if you think authoring a book is only possible with some imagined ideal circumstances, then you may never get started, or you might find your progress is stymied because you are feeling anxiety about the things you think you lack; your perceived shortcomings. Look, instead, at what there is. Thought. Cogitation. Reading. Listening. Man, you have been busy. So, you may not have committed words to the page, but a process is still ongoing. Pondering is the writing, too. Do not forget that now.

This point follows on from the last. You may not write every day – as in get words down on a page – but try to inhabit the world of your book. What might that mean? Perhaps you mull over its characters and plot, read, think about it all on your commute, go for a walk and just let it sit and let your mind freewheel and see what springs up; maybe you keep reading; you look over edits – your own or someone else's – or you could do bits of admin if the urge is that strong. Do your page numbers, check SPAG (spelling and grammar) or write an acknowledgements page: these things can be lovely little boosts and make you feel your book is evolving into an actual THING. Think of the work and the writing as not only being the writing-down, but also of the rumination while you are having a bath, or resting, say. If you do that, you may find your attitude to it shifts, and you might realise you're further along than you thought.

Exercises

A little exercise to do right now. If you do not have a dream… Grab something to write with (if it were me, it would be a not-very-fancy exercise book and a felt-tip pen, I expect). Now, scribble down in any way it comes to you some thoughts about the kind of book you want to write. What would it explore? What themes are in it? Where is it? Don't write what you think you *ought* to be writing, but what you *dream* of doing, because you need to test it on your pulse. *It must make you feel excited.* That will focus the mind. You could also think about what your dream is in publishing:

13

again, consider what you *really* want. Shall I tell you mine? It is to write books that you can see in bookshops, to have at least one of them made into a film and to empower as many people as I possibly can along the way. That's what this book is. I primarily want to be a novelist, but I also want to write other short fiction, features and non-fiction texts: to build a portfolio of varied books. In terms of industry, I want to be with industry professionals who are supportive, open and flexible. Over six years this has not consistently been the case, and, with my everyday concerns, I found it startling and then eviscerating. We will return to looking after and working with this side of things later, as it is all part of the picture.

BUT

Most of all I am going to get totally lost in what I am writing – and we are back to testing on your pulse. This is where everything starts.

I have a second exercise too. I said, *work with what you have*. Well, what *do* you have? And how can you make it better for yourself? Never mind the conditions in which you think you ought to be writing; never mind what you have surmised everyone else is doing. Where can you work? How can you make it a nicer environment for you? This includes things that are soothing if you are prone to anxiety or those troubling *MY WORD MY WRITING IS SHIT WHO AM I KIDDING OH GOD WHAT AM I DOING AND WHAT HAVE I DONE*[2]

---

2 This is my particular hideous train of thought; substitute your own. There is no need to punctuate because hideous trains of thought are unpunctuated.

thoughts which may bubble up as you work. I have essential oils and fake peonies in a vase and music to the rescue on the kitchen table or a desk in my bedroom. Think also about *you*: reflect on your assets, your reading, life experience, the way you see the world, your dialect, accent, phrases specific to you: all that richness and beauty that you are. Think about where you have been – yes, even if it was in your imagination – your sufferings and joys; and know that, with all the stories and the myriad experiences you have, you are extraordinary. And do not tell me you are ordinary, because no one is that – especially not you. In reflecting honestly on what you have, your vision becomes clearer, I think: your vision of who and what you are as a writer. If you can, feel reassured that you don't need a glittering education (readers, I went to Cambridge, albeit from a not-very-good comprehensive, and was sure that everyone there had had a better previous education than me and I still met lots of people – forgive me – who were exam-smart but dumb as soup), or an MA or MFA (although there are many lovely reasons for doing one). I do not have a room of my own, but I have earplugs – or headphones – and a table I gussy up. And I know who I am. I have found my voice. I hope you can hear it speaking to you as I encourage you or remind you to find yours.

Chapter One

Where There's Shit There's Gold

This is a personal essay: how the inside of my head works and what that has to do with my writing and with yours. It's the first – and by far the longest – of a series of essays for you. It's partly about my nan, and I promise that its content is relevant to the feeling and use of this book, so stay with me, but do pop off and get a cup of tea and a snowball[3] if you need to, because this essay is perhaps a little intense. Remember what I said about working with what you have and finding your voice? This essay has those things at its heart, too.

Where there's shit there's gold.

This saying, which you may like, or you may not, is a favourite of mine. It reminds me – reminds *us* – that in tough times, when we are laid low, we need to look for the bright spots; to look for the treasure in the mire. I use this phrase in a variety of contexts, but because we are talking about

3 I realised while writing *The Alchemy* that this word caused confusion. Your snowball in its finest incarnation is made by Tunnocks, and it's a generous-sized and chocolate-covered marshmallow garnished with coconut threads.

writing, since this book is all about writing, including in the context of chronic health problems and difficult stuff, I will look specifically at what this means in that arena.

The saying, by the way, is one of my late grandmother's – and I must ask you to say it with a south Wales accent and slightly theatrically – and she was a working-class woman of limited education and literacy who had a huge number of children, a husband she was not keen on and a tough life. So if *she* could say this about finding gold in shit, then I insist that I can. This essay is partly in her honour, because she was well loved, but had little or no opportunity to follow dreams, such as authoring romantic novels or being on the stage. *I could have been on Broadway*, my nan said to me. I take immense pleasure in knowing that my literary agency is right there on Broadway, and that her granddaughter is doing it partly for her.

But back to the essay on shit and gold.

I carry with me the confusion and weight of complex trauma. My nights were sometimes punctuated with fear as a child – and this explains why I am to this day such an avid reader, for it was always in books that I found solace and company – and I evolved in teenage years, when I was part carer (for ill and dying parents), into part wild child, part eldritch child. That is, I felt separate and odd, but could not embrace the very weirdness of me; and I could not do so for a long time. Books always accepted me in times of intense loneliness and strain; I ran to them when I was dying to tell the outside world that those who were held up as pillars of society were also responsible for demeaning me, subjecting me to slaps, punches and kicks in the sides and the loss of handfuls of hair. Although, when I say I was dying to tell

18

the world, I actually thought I deserved it, and I was told that everyone else would think I had deserved it and so had colluded; moreover, there were lovely times too, so those lovely things seemed to give credence to the fact I deserved it, or sometimes, even, that I had imagined it. You see how confusing that must have been. I do not remember a time when I did not carry around the intense pain of this, and I want to say that I do not, even after good therapeutic care (though extremely late in the day), believe that all sickness can be healed, even that of the mind. We do not all get well, and, in a way, I became freer when I stopped trying to. I understood I had to live with it, and that trauma response had hammered in several responses and appeared to be the reason why I was prone to periods of depression, generalised anxiety, dissociation, panic and OCD. That was not even the whole adventure.

As I became an adult, I still read and read, then taught, read and mothered and was a mentor and volunteer, and read some more, but I did not dare write until I picked up a sharpie and scrawled a title seven years and five months ago. This will sound ridiculous, but *something lit up*. I cannot explain why it happened just then. *Did I finally see the gold?* I was angry and inspired and crying all at once, but, in just a few years, I have written multiple books, across genres and forms. As this book goes to press, I will be starting a PhD by Published Works, which foregrounds my own work. Incredible stuff. This is not me, is it? Surely not. I was told, by the more gaslighting end of the industry, to present as if I had struggled to get published because this was a good story for a woman of a certain age (which meant, I think, an older-than-twenty-five-year-old debut writer), and it reinforced a narrative that was helpful. *Think about that.* It was not that it supported women; it was a helpful marketing tool. In the end, I railed, and things changed there, too: more excitement, energy and crying; more being livid. Why? *Because it was untrue, and the real story was that I had only just started writing.* The point was that, during a long preliminary period I had felt I was nothing – a weirdo, someone who was tolerated, someone of extraordinarily little talent. It was hard for kinder and more expansive minds to puncture this, though wonderful insightful people did try. In short, I was hardwired to feel like a failure, scared of exposure, and I did not have a voice. But it came. And when it did, it was like a torrent – and I can still feel it raging, a river in spate, right now; I can feel it in tender and tingling hands and wrists, my eyes sparkling; a small bomb could detonate next to me and I would carry on tapping away. Once I started writing, I could not stop, and until my toes curl up, I absolutely promise you now that I will not stop. As I said, I took a long time to *start*.

Stay with me: I promise this is relevant to the thrust of this book!

Let me tell you a bit more about the path I had been on before I put pen to paper.

I have, over many years, been introduced as 'the crazy one', 'the mad one,' 'the nutter' and, best of all, 'the weird one I was telling you about' – thereby revealing that they have been talking about your peculiarities behind your back. I used to get terribly upset about this. I have been described this way my entire life and, despite parts of my brain wanting just to be me, weirdo, the other parts yearned for acceptance. This is not a comfortable thing. However, what does 'fitting in' mean? If it means suppressing your character, oddities, imagination, beliefs, and those things that make you you, then this is sad. *You should be you.* Certainly, you ought to reflect on others' responses and needs; check your language and outlook are broad and inclusive – and you ought to self-reflect, because from that stems greater kindness to others. However, if you have earnestly done those things, then come as you are. Because, other than that attention to kindness, detail, and community, FUCK OFF, basically. Weird is great.

Also, weird might be your voice. Your art. It is mine. Trauma and heavy reliance on the world of the imagination do tend to set you a bit apart. That could kill you. It almost killed me twice.

So, I am thinking I have grown into my weird self a bit better. I think I might have raised slightly weird children. One of my offspring was described critically as 'weird' by a teacher on parents' evening, and it was not meant in a positive way. So I quietly said, 'And with that I am going to leave, and maybe we can talk again later after we've considered what might be positive about being weird.'

And I put him in a story, because I like a bit of revenge every now and then.

Because of things that happened to me, I made a few unusual but creative choices: I had a catalogue of imaginary friends well into my teens. This is precisely because I was beaten and scared and gaslit. I made myself into Frida from ABBA because I liked her red hair – my parents had ABBA albums – and my best friend was Agnetha, who had awesome counselling skills. Dolly Parton was another gem in the catalogue (or perhaps gold in the shit), because she was

21

my imaginary mother and big sister. In my late teens, I used to go out with Albert Camus.

When I was sixteen, my best friend was eighty-eight. She got me. She was weird too, and liked bird skulls, tarot and Irish myths and legends. She was a storyteller, God rest her soul. I think that, as with my grandmother, her voice is melded with mine; the one that comes out in writing. I would not have had that had I not been a bit odd. I also wonder if, because I felt lonely and afraid to say things, I listened more – to morbid family stories and myth and legend on both sides. Tales, apocrypha and skewerings that were way too gory to be brought up over sausages and mash. And yet, and yet.

A child at my youngest's primary school recently said to me, 'My mum says you're weird, but I really like you.' Think about that sentence. *You do not know the half of it, love.* There was another time when someone said to me (I remember it well: I was outside the school office, attempting to partially conceal myself behind the bin while trying to hoick my tights up), 'You are clinically insane.' That was someone's ma, too, but directly to me. I was dumbfounded on this occasion because she was smiling, and I was a bit stuck on the word 'clinically', because as far as I knew she was an interior designer. It might have been the fact I was partially concealed behind the bin that prompted the comment, but it was more likely a sense, after having made various observations and tours of me, of having to express a dislike of something... off; odd; eldritch. To spit it out – as if you thought you had put a chocolate in your mouth and realised it was a rock, or some poo. I had started writing by this point, though, so, instead of suppressing tears at her laughing, callous comment, I decided I might have her exit pursued by a bear in something.

So when I found the gold, it did not take away the shit – neither then nor now – but it did help me find recourse so that I could recover: now I could take revenge by having (a version of) the mouth that spawned those words heartily eaten by an evil pie-maker in my short-story volume, *Famished*.[4] Do you think me awful? I really do find it a relief from tension and unkindness to write someone out and occasionally have them in the wrong place when the kraken rises.

And yes, maybe I do look 'clinically insane' to some people. I dress in a funny mixture of Victoriana and sports kit, and I have a tattoo in Latin. I carry my chickens about, crooning to them. I was reading Dostoevsky to them the other day – although they prefer Flaubert, and the shorter prose at that. Do you see where I am going with this? Because of my past, and because of the problems I have had and will always have, I spot inspiration in unexpected places, and my oddity – born, I believe, of necessity and separation from the healthy mass – looks for conversations in unusual places. I cannot wait to start a conversation with the man who whispers and gurgles to his rooks, the lady who has a tiny glittering altar outside her house or the man who crosses the road every time he sees the local priest. I have a theory that maybe, if you are a bit odd, you notice more. And maybe – even more radically – you notice people who might be a bit marginalised but with whom you could have a great chat and suddenly everyone there is having a better day. You do that because you have been so

4 *Famished* (London: Influx Press, 2020).

hurt and so lonely and feel it to your core, and perhaps it makes you more responsive to others.

What do *you* think? That is the point, and it took me years to figure it out: what do *you* think? (You superb weirdo.)

I think, then, that my grandmother's saying was right. There have been long days and nights, with cortisol firing and flashbacks; frightening recurrent dreams, and in the day, I ordered and reordered like a talisman and thus OCD came to stay, with all its persistent, intrusive thoughts: as a primary-school child, I would have to go and tell a person a bad thought I had about them to stop the bad thing happening to them. It was not even a bad thought, just words that occurred and had not even coalesced into a pattern. Either way, this is not normal behaviour by any stretch. Not the intrusive thought, but its persistence and the fact that I really did believe that, if not surrendered to source, calamity would befall. Somewhere, embedded in my psyche, were the words of my mother repeated early and thus lodged; I did not know how to tease them out. I had been led to believe that I was a burden, that *I* was the calamity, that *I* was the bringer of harm.

Where is the gold in that shit? There was none; not then. But one day I realised that all along I had believed in the transformative power of words; I had just believed in it the wrong way, and had yet to connect this kind of magical think-ing with the magic I felt wrapped up inside books, sucking on words, transported. That was the gold, and it also came later, when I found my voice. Not only because I had spectacular anecdotes, but because I was quite capable of being in my imagination and creating something, inhabiting it passion-ately. I had learned that exceedingly early and, about seven ears ago, when I found my voice, it was what helped me make books: all that mental-health adventure and the horrible events which preceded and accompanied it all, now *that* was threaded through narratives and made richly coloured.

My thinking goes rat-a-tat-rat-a-tat all day long; allusive; solving problems with quotations; snatches of song if need be. It is how I manage things; but I am also always making stories and seeing links. I wish I had had the confidence to write books earlier – but it is all coming out now. That is because of the weird I am, you see. *It is liberated.* And partly because of the shit: I take the worst moments from dissociative episodes I have had, and images, rhythms, and repetitions I recall and feel from the psychotic episode I had before one of my breakdowns. I am not – please do not misunderstand me – saying that suffering is a path to art, because I have always found that suggestion trite and offensive. But I could not escape, and I had no one to tell. And I could not get better – *I am not better* – so I have tried to mould it and form it into something I can share with others.

Here is the thing: we are all a patchwork of oddities, and everyone really is an outsider in their questing and difficult experience. We all hurt, and we all have emotional problems. How much better to channel those into something creative which might absorb and bring pleasure to others than to suck that pain in and turn it outwards by planting it on others, manipulating and gaslighting them instead as a displacement activity because you hurt inside. So find your weird, explore it in writing, as I have done and will continue to do. Ultimately, just be you: you are perfect, and just as you were meant to be, memento mori, spoon-collecting, fancy-dress you. Perfect you in pain, not fixed, sick, screwed up and shat on, but indescribably beautiful and incandescently talented.

Remember: where there's shit there's gold. That gold is your work. That gold is also, my darling, *YOU*.

So, there we have it. MY GOD YOU CONTAIN MULTITUDES HAVE YOU EVEN REALLY LOOKED AT YOU RECENTLY – and maybe you just don't know it yet. Did you have a tough start or middle? Or do you think you are approaching the end of it all and your creativity, your ability to set down a story and turn it into a book are gone? *Challenge all that.* Or, if I may, let this book challenge all that. The imagination is there, waiting to be ignited, but you need to start by being comfortable with your ridiculous self, your hurting, silly self. Revisit the mean things said to you, the things that went wrong and channel it all. If not the events, then the energy: burn some fury off, why don't you? This is, to reiterate, partly what I mean about alchemy, and partly what I think of in terms of the quotation used as an epigraph which you skipped over (I saw you there). The one is that the science of alchemy was the change of base metals into gold; the other that sorrow transforms and remakes you, but from that may come something new; from the dark comes the light. Whatever your experience, take from it. If there are elements which are really, really tough, I wonder if we can take some energy and some anger from that. Like I said, perfect you in pain, not fixed, sick, screwed up and shat on, but indescribably beautiful and incandescently talented.

Remember: where there's shit there's gold. That gold is your work. That gold is also, my darling, *YOU*.

An Exercise

Be honest with yourself about whether any of this is triggering or likely to lower your mood to the point where work becomes more difficult. Promise you will do this first?

OK, in terms of material for a book or developing what you already have I want you to lounge about now with a hot drink and possibly a weighted blanket (this is me – I am telling you what I would do). You may have anger to burn or grief as a form of energy. We will go with that – I know that this is what I have done. Think about some curious incidents that have happened to you. Can these be part of the story of your book, or integrated into the story in some way? Yes – that might work for autobiographical fiction, but think not only in terms of sketching out your own experience: put your experience in the life of someone else and imagine how they might deal with it – someone whom you perceive as radically different from you, perhaps? Give it a different ending or route to get there. I have found that offering someone else – a character I made – my experience felt like a safer route into a book for me, because it distanced me; and, in the spirit of gentle productivity – at the core of which is using what you have – I found good material there. Spend just ten minutes today putting your experiences in the life of another; shift context, country, anything you like. Let's see what happens.

And by the way, while some might refer to this as 'literary recycling', I have actually done this; the themes I explore in my memoir are looked at again, but in a different time and place and with very different people (and in one case species) in my latest novel. There are germs of what I already have, but the story is fresh and new.

Please have faith in yourself, too – and the stories you tell.

Chapter Two

A Writing Day

What might it look like – perfect, or, for the purposes of this book, fractured and imperfect?

This will be a difficult one, because I cannot know your circumstances, and some of these descriptions will, therefore, exist in a broad sweep – but I shall try. You might be at work all day or working part-time; you might be away from home, or perhaps you cannot leave your home or are just feeling sad and low on energy.

Let me describe today, the 17th of March 2022, to you. First, I have a three-quarter day off, but I am teaching two after-school classes later. I am more energetic than of late because I have been sleeping better, owing to increased pain relief and a better relaxation and stretching routine in bed. These things mean I am managing the anxiety over one of my sons, who has been ill over a protracted period, somewhat better. Life is still frequently sad and challenging, partly because health services in the UK are so heavily triaged, and it can be heartbreaking failing, again and again, to access help. Still, I know that during the day I will have bubbles of anxiety, and I have to attend to and work with and through those. I had to shop earlier and sort out medical things; now I am at my desk. I will probably have been at my desk for two hours in total. In forty minutes, my youngest will come home from primary school, so better check if there are snacks and so on, and so on. And I am supposed to rest for a period each day to help me better relax and manage pain and fatigue.

How, amongst these things, did writing occur? First I had to make up my mind to enjoy what I could do and push away anxiety about what I was not producing. That is why, first of all, I am writing this and not the memoir I also need to work on. Because the mood was right and I was working with and alongside the day. Here I am working, at my desk, and telling you what I am doing right now in that work, so it's an economy of sorts. When I went to Lidl earlier, I had some index cards with me because I knew I was going to tell you later in this book about leaning in and listening and people-watching and eavesdropping. Before I went in, I sat in the car and I had my mug of tea with me, and I sat for a few minutes, being on my own – I am frequently interrupted at home – and I thought about what I had written on the cards (we will return to that), and also let my mind just freewheel a bit on chapter topics.

Here is the magic. If you let yourself go in a bit of imaginative freewheeling, it is amazing what comes out. I looked at the cards again – on them were prompts for things to look out for: folk, ideas, characters, conversations; lives. People are endlessly fascinating, and so is the interaction between them. So when I went into the shop, I was doing my shopping but also, gently and slowly, thinking about the process of everyday observation. And do you know what? It was for a later chapter of this book, but something happened which gave me an idea for another piece of writing in another book I've been humming and hawing about. I thought about the interplay between two characters in a different way. Do you see that this is quite a bit of thought, in its own way, and in an unexpected form, perhaps?

I needed to rest when I got home, though not for long, and decided to read what is, without doubt, my favourite book on writing: Francine Prose's *Reading Like a Writer*.[5] I looked at the beginning where she explains that she teaches – and I think this is very similar to my own taste – in detail, word by word, sentence by sentence. I continued being at work there, on the bed, legs up on an exercise ball, rotating ankles, and looked at her thoughts on detail. I have read this book twice, but came to it again today, and I believe that a lot of work comes by restfully reading something that is constructed so clearly and is a prompt to close reading.

Prose describes how she reads closely, word by word, sentence by sentence; that she considers each and every deceptively minor decision the writer has made. I love this! You try it too and luxuriate, rest in it, in that moment. Prose explains that while it's impossible to recall every source of inspiration and instruction she received, she can certainly remember the novels and stories that brought revelations, describing them as wells of beauty and pleasure and also as textbooks: they were private tutorials in the art of writing fiction. I find this so exciting. Read closely and critically, and try to lose your self-consciousness about whether you are doing it the right way or not and feel glad, as I do, that reading is your finest teacher.[6]

---

5 Francine Prose, *Reading Like a Writer: A Guide for People Who Love Books and for Those Who Want to Write Them* (London: Union Books, 2006).

6 'Close Reading', *Reading Like a Writer*, pp. 3–4.

So here is a crucial point about gentle productivity. Excellent teaching is explained here and elaborated upon with a wealth of detail and reading examples for you. If you were to spare ten minutes a day first reading this text and thereafter, or alongside, if you can (I believe that good writers are readers, first of all, and often voracious ones), just picking up a fiction book and looking at the first two paragraphs, or even a page at random and really pondering how something is done, 'putting every word on trial for its life' as Francine has it, much would be learned and studied, and it could all inform how you write your book and feed in to the care with which you approach its construction. This is efficient, but it is also care for you. Today, my hands and legs hurt; pain kept me awake overnight, so I know there is a limit to what I can do: this is what I chose with my limits.

I would like to offer some more thoughts which have comforted me deeply, and which I have always instinctively known to be true yet had not articulated – someone else got there first. In *A Still Life*[7] Josie George writes brilliantly about action and caring for oneself, making decisions and being clear of every step. When my health worsened, partly because of Long Covid and because I was caring for a very ill son, with no external support over an extended period, this book was an immense comfort to me. Importantly, it helped me write more, and that is perhaps surprising for a book which is about stillness and small actions.

Ah, but there are surprises along the way, and perhaps we have ingested some fibs about what productivity – or action, for that matter – actually *are*. George writes that there is a

---

7 Josie George, *A Still Life* (London: Bloomsbury, 2021).

huge amount of power in taking ownership of one's actions, so that every step taken, every decision made, can have an effect, even if that is only on oneself, even short bursts. And when one has seen that effect, how can they continue to hear that they are lazy? How can they believe themselves less than anyone else?[8]

Isn't this the most comforting and, in its way, radical, rebellious thing? I have had to learn and relearn such things, but in these little bursts of reading and thinking I've described, much gets done, and my quiet mind is thinking them over, thinking abouts words, phrases, punctuation, the gaps between words, the grace notes, if you like, working away: don't ever underestimate those kind machinations; those gentle ruminations. Decide what you will do, then, for your book, and dedicate yourself to it – and remember, as you go, George's advice: believe in gentle actions in creativity – the small choices made; they're not made to prove oneself but to keep one moving forwards, ready to greet life and look whatever it throws at you straight in the eye.

Keep that in mind if you manage a rest and read, a short burst of book activity in between rest times: have faith that you are nurturing a quiet power here.

By the end of today, with two rests and focused reading bursts, giving myself some pep talks, the shopping trip with a bit of time in the car, the cards, the book problem solved and the people-watching, quite a lot went down. At teatime, I wrote this chapter. I wasn't expecting that!

---

8 See *A Still Life*, pp. 142–143.

An Exercise

Might you get one of those little books of index cards in pastel shades for a few quid? Or a notebook, or some other small thing to write in? Have it with you when you are away from the home – or next to you, if it is not possible for you to be away from the home. Something to do today is to note on these cards some things to look out for – to lean in to and really, fully notice. I did this in Lidl. You can do it wherever you are. In whatever little periods of time you have. I should add that of course we all went through – are going through – a pandemic, and more people are still shielding for safety than many realise, right? I also understand you may need to be at home for any number of reasons; I just had two years when I had to be here and on alert. As I was saying, notice. On your key cards – or do this with voice notes instead if you like or need to – it might say, as concisely as possible:

1. Overhear a conversation and imagine the lives of the people having it. Create a backstory or a future story for them.
2. Notice the textures of things. The difference and range. If you had gone to a shop, it might be bread or fruit, floor, or ceiling, but it could also be wall and door; the ways in which light shifts and varies; and this is something I have done at home. Then, ponder how any of those things might be represented in a different setting. This has been helpful to me because I was writing a short story, or maybe because I had faith it would feed into my book; and for points 1 & 2, I might then aim to note down my responses to the things I observed.

3. I include this because you might have a specific thing you are thinking about – say, a sticking point in your novel. I realised that in the book which has just gone out on agency submission there was not enough change and development. (When I say I realised, I mean my agent pointed it out!) So here is what I did. During the Lidl trip, I had on my index card some thoughts about how I was feeling before I went into the shop. Then, when I'd stuffed everything in the boot, I sat with one of those Bakewell tart 'healthy' (ho ho!) bars by the till and my travel cup of slightly stewed Yorkshire tea and thought about what had changed by the time I had come out: mood, physical self, cognitions. THAT helped me think about progression and narrative for a human being. The following day, in little bursts of activity, I put comment bubbles on manuscript, and they were all WHAT HAS CHANGED, aided and abetted by my thoughts about my own psychology in the Lidl trip before and after.

Some might laugh at that. *No. That would not work. It could not.* PAH.

I did it. I have done it frequently. Here is the baton for you. Or your Bakewell tart bar, in fact.

Chapter Three

Exercises for and Thoughts on

Writer's Block

Let me suggest a range of things here, tried and evaluated, and I would love to know how you got on. Let me reiterate some things first, however, and these are about how you might be feeling, as I do think this is inextricably bound up with writing a book – writing any sentence, maybe – and frequently with how we are when things grind to a halt.

I understand writing can be a tender process. I have often felt like an underachiever, so putting a book out there was a bit like going out to a busy high street wearing only underwear AND I DID NOT EVEN HAVE MY BEST PANTS ON. Oh, no: the old, comfortable pants, a bit frayed, elastic gone. Oh, *you* know. People pointed, stared, and said, OH MY GOD and also, LOOK AT THE STATE OF THOSE PANTS, A BIT FRAYED AND THE ELASTIC GONE. I've found myself fearing exposure and others' opinions, wanting to be liked (this I am SURE is because my parents didn't like me very much) and also a sense of shame – who did I think I was? – and added to this the sense I had ingested that writing was not an actual job, but always a hobby and generally performed by dilettantes. I could write another book just on that last point!

But look.

Writing a book might be a long-cherished ambition and bound up with how you feel about yourself – I recognise that – so helping ourselves to see a broader picture and connect with others (it doesn't need to be face-to-face) really helps. The industry is brutal, if that's where you're headed, so forming a little community gives you a carapace and blunts your (relative) isolation. I tackle specific tips, too. If the book is feeling too close to your own emotion, focus on its technical side and go back and look at sentence structure and line editing. Also, reconsider what writing a book is; what productivity is. The bulk of your book is thinking and pondering; it is reading and cogitation. So I encourage you not to panic about word count and about stops, starts, complete halts and pauses and deciding your book is shit – instead, I hope it will quell your anxiety to see how much is going on all the time. If you manage chronic illness and have only spoonfuls of energy to be meted out, you have to do it like that. If you are a carer, the same. The books you see and which are coming in 2023 are all made in far-from-ideal conditions, and really this is what clarified a lot of thoughts in this book. So be aware that this sense of vulnerability is OK and does not make you a neurotic amateur. Then, I hope you feel soothed by the idea that, even when you halt, the book goes on. Try to see the hiatus as only one part of the work and, in regulating your thoughts on that, hopefully you will be able to go back to the writing, putting words on the page again very soon.

If you decide to take a break, your book is not gone: it is waiting for you to come back; so do not be fearful of that. Be kind in what you say to yourself, and be your own best advocate. That is, good self-talk. Reframe what has happened, so that, rather than telling yourself your book has failed and you are a creative dud, you tell yourself that you are going to walk away for a while – because that is sensible, and what a clever idea it is to be sensible and kind to yourself.

I began with pants, so let us end with them. I do not recommend going out only in your underwear to test the water and your growing confidence, but I tell you this: if you love those pants (the ones where the elastic's gone), wear them. Be you. Also, if I may pass on the following tip: pants are not really that important. If someone really fancies you, the sight of those dilapidated but comfortable numbers is not going to cool things at the bedroom door. This has nothing to do with writing, yet my wont is to encourage you to be comfortable with doubt, mess and the stop-start nature of creativity, to be gentle with yourself, so maybe, on reflection, it *does*.

Exercises

Fear not… Try one, some or all.

Everyone gets stuck – of course they do – so don't fret about that. However, what if you cannot commit a word to the page at all and feel a bit panicky about it? Here is a strategy.

1. Go and do something entirely different for a while. See if you can write something else – something that has nothing to do with your main project. Sometimes it

may feel like it's your overall ability to create, to think, that's the problem, but frequently it's just connected with the task in hand.

2. Authoring a novel? Try a poem, short story, opinion piece: whatever takes your fancy. FUN FACT. I did this with book three. I started writing a short story and kept going. It ended up as a published book. After a while, try going back to the other book – sneak up on it!

3. Pick up a pen or pencil and begin doodling, scribbling, drawing shapes and cross-hatching. You are relaxing as you do this. If you want, this can be done on your computer. Now, introduce a few words… they can be random at first – you are freeing the stuck bits – so just let this do its work. Now introduce a few words or phrases from your novel, with intermittent doodling and more of the same, then back to the words.

4. At some point, you might pop your computer on – or, if you write in longhand, stay right where you are – and, wherever you left off, begin again, just writing random words or recognisable phrases. Have them in a different font, because you are going to cross this out later, and we don't want to miss anything. Now try to shift towards a continuation of what you were writing for your novel, and hopefully you are a little more relaxed and unstuck? If not, repeat the whole process and try again.

5. Here is another idea. Sometimes it might be easier to say the words, so try using the function on your phone or even an old-fashioned Dictaphone[9] (I happen to

---

9 You probably know this, but you can use the dictation facilities on your phone readily. I have some hearing loss and, while the link I am about to share is for others who do, it's also a useful guide to apps for dictation. Otter is the one I like. https://rnid.org.uk/information-and-support/technology-and-products/speech-to-text-smartphone-apps/

love them, and have had mine for twenty-five years!) or read-aloud facility on your laptop (these are likely already on your laptop, but if not, as long as it is above a certain specification, you can install it). Feeling better?

6. I mentioned doing something different. If you are stuck, feeling thwarted, or if your confidence is shaking in its boots, a practical activity when you are not actively focused on the task in hand can really unlock things. If you are able to get out, pushing a shopping trolley up and down the aisles works for me (obviously while shopping), or fixing things – doing a small repair. Something where you are using your hands to build, mend or collect. The key thing is to mitigate stress and anxiety around the blockage, whatever kind it is, so that you free up your mind.

7. Another simple but effective strategy is something I've seen recommended by many: leave the work and walk away from it; if the option presents itself, you might then talk a plot problem through with someone you trust. That might be your husband, your current lover if you're a bit racier, a pal – or anyone you feel would have insight. I would add that, if the issue is one of plot, or a thorny issue with a character, asking on socials is good. Use the hashtags #amwriting #amediting and #writingcommunity and ten to one some marvellous ideas will come in.

8. Most of all, breathe in through the nose and out through the mouth SLOWLY and remember that this happens to everyone and to varying degrees. Even at its worst, being frozen, thinking you cannot complete the task or even take another step forward, this is natural. Hideous, yes, but natural. I hope that thought brings comfort and just a little relaxation.

Chapter Four

Thoughts on Eavesdropping

*People are incredible, bizarre and fascinating. How does
subtle leaning in, lapping up and noticing make books?
Observations in Lidl and other joints.*

I was a strange and shy little girl. I still am that person. Let
me tell you a story.

Something happened, and I cannot quite pin down when.
I am not sure that I am actually shy: I am neurodivergent
and had an immediate family who managed to convince
me that I was a little weirdo and that anyone I met would
think that and not want to accept me. It did get a little better
sometimes, but the damage was done and I did not know
how to make it better. But gradually I began to haul myself
out of silence and into focusing on others, and I began to talk
to people I met. I found my peers generally intimidating in
secondary school, and often at university too – I am not sure
I would now, if you put me back there, but I am stronger and
clearer these days – but the people I began to talk to were on
the bus and in shops, at the doctor's: I discovered there are
people who like a chat everywhere.

This was a revelation. They seemed to like talking to me, too. I liked hearing their stories and news, and as I got older, and had children, the interactions increased. My boys would say, 'How do you know those people?' and I would say, 'I don't.'

We're talking about the women on the tills in Home Bargains. The guy who runs the funny old (and brilliant) electrical shop in town. The woman who had a greeting job in Asda.

People. Everyday, ordinary, but so far from it, just like you.

People love to talk. Even shy people – or people who think they are shy! Talk to them; talk back: modulate how you respond, taking cues as much as you can – but look: I am a funny old soul, socially clumsy and a bit nervous, and if I can do it, you can, if you want. If you can do this, your world will expand, and it is entirely possibly everyone leaves the room feeling better because, of course, you never know how lonely or isolated someone else may feel.

From your conversations and enlarging world may come stories, and that's why I am including these thoughts in *The Alchemy*. If you are out and about and need inspiration, lean in, chat and eavesdrop as lives, feelings and interactions reveal themselves.

I am going to change the details here, so no one is identifiable, but there is a man in a local store who, every year, reads *A Christmas Carol* aloud to himself. He starts in November and wouldn't miss it for the world. He's not a bookish man, but this is a bedrock of his life, he told me, and we talked about my love of Dickens. How did this even happen? Because when I went into my bag to get my wallet, he caught sight of a copy of *Great Expectations* in there and said, 'Is that Dickens? I have only read one Dickens, although I know about others…' And on it went.

In another shop is a woman who has been very sad about one of her older children, and we ended up comparing notes. Basically, she shared that her child was lonely and frustrated and possibly also very bright, but she did not know how to help. She told me she was radically different from her child and could not understand how to help, and she did not really value herself and – tears were pricking my eyes here – she had wasted her life and had little education and was not very bright. That is a lot to unpick. I shared my story, and we were nodding in complicity. I don't believe anyone had been complimenting that lovely and loving woman.

Both those people contributed to the novel I just wrote – not in plot, but in feeling. The storyteller who peoples his world just for himself; the mother loving but baffled by her child and feeling that she could not be an example. When I have to go out and about, I try to spend a few minutes mulling over what has happened and the conversations that have occurred.

There is much you will notice and ingest just from being observant. I must, as with talking to people, advise discretion and possibly caution, but it is not hard to be going about your business and be watching the way others interact in shops, cafés, the library, benefits office, doctor's surgery; in your workplace; amongst your neighbours. Notice body language and gestures. Be alive to others' conversations, which can be full of amazing detail. A little while ago, I popped into Sainsbury's on the way home and, in the crisps-and-snacks aisle, someone was talking into their mobile in a muffled voice, phone half up their sleeve, snivelling and crying. I saw it and pondered what to do, but walked on, shooting a smile across; a few minutes' later I came back down the same aisle to get to the till and the person was still there, still crying, but now off the phone. I asked her if she was OK – was there anything I could do? Her eyes widened and her face broke into a broad smile, and she said, 'Love, thanks. Honestly, I had brilliant news, and I just couldn't take it in. I am in a right state.' It was not what I thought it was at all.

There is a story in that: a situation which was vastly different from what you thought.

Or was it a situation that was very different from what you thought, and you got caught up in it?

Or a situation which appeared to be very different from what you thought?

Or was it a situation which was being acted out and was, in fact, a lure to catch you in some way, in some form – and now why would that happen?

Or was it witnessed by several people and each was told a different story, or had a different perception of the event, or saw a different section of it – and they all converged on the scene at one point? And then what happened – as in the beginning of Ian McEwan's *Enduring Love* – as everyone runs to the point when the hot air balloon is falling from the sky and there is a boy in the balloon and a man attached to the basket…

As I say, *then* what happened?

An Exercise

Go into a shop; really look at what is seen, heard and observed. And you will do so perhaps more acutely than you have before, because it's so easy to go about chores and everyday demands and not really pay attention. Or we sail through them with earbuds in and we have been dislocated from present reality (not that there's anything wrong with that).

When you come out, think about three things which made an impression on you and consider why that is – because they were unusual, perhaps? Or because you are surprised you had not noticed something before? As well as considering what you observed, do you have any thoughts on what you could not understand? The mystery of human encounter is always fascinating. Did you, for example, notice two people together and find it impossible to tell (admittedly you didn't have much time because if you did, you'd look like a stalker – again, I am advising caution in your manoeuvres) what connection existed between them? With some people you can see they are a couple and are relaxed in one another's company. You might – and I apologise if this sounds peculiar to you, but I have already explained that I am socially gauche, so please bear with me – notice how tactile they are with each other, or from their intensity and consistency of eye contact you might surmise that they have amazing sex. (Told you.) But let me share an encounter which spawned another encounter and led, in fact, to a Twitter[10] conversation and then a short story.

---

10 We know it is slowly becoming X – 'Blaze your glory' (Dear Lord), but the terminology used is that which people are currently more used to.

This is a tale about passive-aggressive communication – all names and places have been changed to protect the individuals involved, although the fact that they were talking about varieties of dog food has not been altered, because the dog was clearly involved in some way in this lexical tug of war and well-heeled domestic despair.

Couple standing by the dog food in Asda.

'Barry, I'll get kibble for him, shall I?'

'Sure.'

'What do you mean, "Sure"? Do you mean yes or no, Barry?'

Sighing noise. 'I meant "Sure", which is why I said it.'

'So, you're annoyed with me, right?'

'No, I just don't really care what kind of dog food we get.'

'There's no need to be so irritable with me – and especially in public, Barry.'

'OK.'

'What do you mean, *OK*? Do you think I ought to get some other kind of dog food? Tinned. Should I get tinned dog food?'

'Just get the kibble, Sandra, ALL RIGHT?'

'There's no need to be so arsey, for fuck's sake, Barry.'

'Look, Sandra, I don't really have any say in what we buy anyway, do I?'

'I KNEW IT!'

Two sighing noises.

Kibble is thrown into the trolley, plus a few tins of dog food.

I was actually browsing in the freezer section while this was going on and lingered over the labelling. *Hmm. Is this really gluten-free?*

A voice chirped up from beside me. 'Were you listening to Sandra and Barry too?'

'What? Hello. Sandra and Barry – who are they? No. Well, yes. Do you know them?'

'Oh no, but I often shop in here, and they have these weird little altercations all over the shop, and I think it's part of their routine. I think they enjoy it.'

We had two different perspectives now. Plus, Sandra and Barry, in the eight minutes in which I had known of them, had acquired a backstory, and it was interesting. I was thinking about love and the many shapes it has, and domesticity, aggression and routine. About how the self can be subsumed in a relationship but, crucially, I wondered, as I stood by the cauliflower-cheese grills (not gluten-free, obviously) if I had been seeing them wrong.

So: see what happens. Perhaps it will illuminate part of your story, your book – or start or create a new one; maybe in observations and leaning-in of this kind you will evolve a collection of themed short stories on loneliness, love in various incarnations, on supermarkets as strange parallel worlds (going a bit liminal there), on domesticity and, perhaps, what happens when it intersects with the outside world – and by extension is reacted to by others.

An individual for whom I had been a support teacher came out of mainstream education and into home education, where we met again as I helped set things up for GCSE exams. He was extremely interested in creative writing and, as you may possibly know, creative writing as a GCSE and A-level subject was discontinued a few years ago as part of an overhaul, and partly on the basis that it was skills-based, not knowledge based. There remain some strands of creative writing in the suite of English GCSEs and A levels, and that is it. I have always tried to encourage broad reading and creative writing for leisure where I could. But this lad: he had time and space now during the working/school week and came bounding in: 'I've been going for walks during the day and I just never realised!' I asked what he'd never realised, and he went on to describe the people he saw on his (urban) walks. They were people he didn't think he saw at weekends or during the evenings when he had previously been out and about. 'They were, I think, people who are marginalised. People who are really old,[11] people in groups, people who don't look very well.' He told me that, during this new time and in acquiring new perspectives, he had begun keeping a diary and turning what he wrote in the diary into sketches, inventing backstories and imagining lives. 'I am going to write all this up at some point,' he said.

I will leave that with you. Teaching teenagers is brilliant. They generally know more than adults.

Here are just a few more exercises – out and about, but also if you cannot get out. These are further things to get you thinking when out and about or just pondering at home. Look at what people are doing and, also, how they are interacting with one another. Look for subtle signs and ponder them; remember that communication is not only verbal, but drawn from many extra-linguistic features, from paralanguage. That is, gestures, facial expressions.

---

11 He was sixteen. I assumed at first that he meant people who were about eighty, but he could have meant the over-thirties, now I think about it. Or people close to death. Like me. Hopeless cases.

At the bus stop, on a station or on a train, in the car, while walking along – really look carefully at the people around you.

What is the expression on someone's face? What do you think their mood might be?

Do you notice any intriguing interpersonal behaviour? The way they respond to strangers,

for example – on a station platform, in a shop.

How do different people speak to cashiers? What does that suggest to you about

character?

Do you notice that some people are solitary in a social space and some people interact?

Why is that interesting?

At home. In bed, say. Or just sitting for a moment. This is about you, now.

IMPORTANT

IF IT MAKES YOU FEEL VULNERABLE AT THE MOMENT, SKIP THIS ONE.

---

1. Which situations with other people – broadly – make you feel uncomfortable and why?
2. Can you think of a situation when you felt truly at ease; happy? It might have been an unexpected or unusual situation. That is interesting!
3. Think about a time when you met a fascinating person. What was so fascinating about them?
4. Have you ever formed an impression of someone's character and discovered you were wrong?

5. In a book, poem or story you have read, or maybe a play you've seen, which character or characters did you find compelling and why?

6. What is your favourite landscape? It might be urban; it might be rural. Whatever it is, think about the place – or type of place – whether it's a dunescape or a station platform, and what it is that beguiles you; what it is that makes you want to explore this place or kind or place, OR what feelings it engenders in your book? Ponder this one.

Remember that everything here is material for a new work or can assist you in the deepening of what you already have because you are thinking about character, motive, personality; you are pondering context, atmosphere and mood. All this you are doing while on your way somewhere else. If you have a notebook with you, you could be writing any of this down, but if that feels like too much – on your commute, say – just let yourself be open to contemplation and reverie, keeping these questions in mind, and retrieve your thoughts later. There's a downloadable resource on the Alchemy forum of all the questions I have put to you here, and you can print off and have them to look at while you go. It will be at once unremarkable and richly rewarding.

Try it. That is *The Alchemy* at work.

Chapter Five

Taking a Writing Walk

Drawing creativity and hard words from that.

We cannot all move very much. Or walk. Perhaps we used to be able to, but now we are tired. *Perhaps, perhaps.* I wanted to think about this for *The Alchemy*, because I cannot in all consciousness have a whole chapter that huge numbers of writers and aspiring writers cannot do or would find difficult. I had Long Covid, and as I write, I am much recovered, but two summers ago I discovered what fatigue was for the first time – not tiredness, or sleep deprivation, but a bone-crushing feeling. As if I could not move; like a weight was pressing down on me and my limbs would not work. When they did, all I wanted to do was lie down again. It did get better very gradually, but brought with it a new understanding of the state of things borne by so many who manage chronic illness, be it ME, CFS, fibromyalgia or something else. I have learned from pals new and old in those communities all about managing fatigue, resting – *good* resting – and economies of movement; and about consciously choosing my next act, my next movement. I learned a little more about thinking small and, because my eldest son was also desperately ill during this period, I applied it to my own distress in order to alleviate that and to better help my own child.

What, you ask, has any of this to do with writing? Because during all this time I was writing books, and two were published during lockdown when my health and my eldest son's health were on the floor. I got better at focus, gentle movement forward and clearer thought, and it all accrued. Also, I timed movement and thought – and by thought, I mean thought about my book. So I would be going for a short stroll – I got tired so quickly – or trying to do some stretching exercises I had formerly learned in Pilates and yoga, and as I did them, really thinking about the movement I made, I would frequently be unrolling a thought about part of a short story or the novel I was working on. For example, I knew that a key setting in *The Zebra and Lord Jones*[12] had to be a quay on the Daugleddau Estuary in Pembrokeshire, because it was deeply atmospheric, felt absolutely right and it was where my grandmother and great grandmother had lived. A magical place of mud, deep woods and water. So I tried to *feel* that place, bringing up all its sensory elements so I could smell the salt-mud, hear the whirling sea birds and feel the smooth stepping stones across the tidal stream on my bare feet. I needed to know, well away from there, the rough feel of the wrack and kelp on my fingers, the pop of bladderwrack. I was lost to those small thoughts as I made physical movements. I had to do the same with three areas of London. I know the city fairly well, but it is still not hugely familiar to me, so my bringing up of knowledge of detail

---

12 *The Zebra and Lord Jones* (London: Renard Press, 2023).

– stone, pavement, smells – depended partly on film and books. Dwelling on those things, seeing the images in my mind's eye and feeling sensations of what I knew, as well as what I had ingested from someone else's observances – now that was exciting, partly because it was less familiar.

Again, I did it alongside gentle movements. Sometimes I was physically moving and sometimes I just made the movements in my head. I understand this is a technique known as 'mind sculpture' where you perform something – a movement or a situation – in your mind to rehearse it, to practise it. There were times, during the summer of 2020, when I felt weights on my chest. I had Covid early, and it has taken me at least eighteen months to recover, and my chest still aches! I wanted to fight the exhaustion, but I learned from those who manage this in daily living that this does not work, so the walks I could not go on, and I went on lying down. When I was there, in my lying-down walk, I was writing my novel. Sometimes – because the summer of 2020 was my annus horribilis in which my third novel and first short-story collection fairly sank during lockdown – as well as these full-on sensory and imaginary walks, I was dealing with thoughts of resentment, upset and many things over these two books. Clearly not rational and, frankly, rather self-indulgent, but I had to let those feelings sit and worm their way out before I tried to squash them altogether. Also, I needed to find enough energy to keep talking about my April 2020 novel and start talking more about my September 2020 short-story collection.

Phew.

I did a lot of this horizontal and rehearsed in my head, when I was not walking on the upper Daugleddau (in my head), so I could practise writing my next novel, including imagining hard details like the shape of zebra hooves in estuary mud: it was all work.

I stumbled across another fascinating and resonant idea in an essay by the writer and artist Alec Finlay, who creates the most beautiful things while being very open about the impact of ME/CFS on his life.[13] He compares managing chronic illness and wanting to walk and not being able to with playing Patience. He explains that just because someone wants something – in this case to walk – it doesn't make it possible; what matters is what the person can manage or imagine. For some people it might be possible to scale great mountains whilst on crutches, and they are surely due the medals they're awarded; but for others this isn't possible in reality – so for those who can't walk, the alternative is to travel in the imagination – to follow paths and ascents in one's mind's eye. Following this realisation, he came up with the concept of the 'Proxy Walk'. For this art project, one person chose a walk they used to love, when they were able to walk; meanwhile, the other participant does the walk for them. Agreeing to do so at exactly the same time, the two write down their experiences – one writing as they walk and the other describing the route from memory. Finlay goes on to say that, due to the pandemic, his role has changed from walker to imaginer. He also nods to a fellow artist who 'gifts walks' – going on walks for other women who aren't able to – and a nurse in a Perthshire care home who goes on walks on the behalf

---

13 Alec Finlay, 'On Not Walking, Part II', Poetry Foundation (22 December 2020). https://www.poetryfoundation.org/harriet-books/2020/12/on-not-walking-part-ii.

of the home's residents. The point of these projects, he clarifies, is recognising limits and offering new possibilities.

For me, when I was too unwell to walk further than the end of a garden before I needed to rest, when at the beach I could not explore because fatigue pressed down on me and I had no choice but to lie down, I asked my husband and youngest to do a proxy walk for me. Sometimes they went to places I did not yet know, but I imagined their surroundings while they saw them. When they came back, we talked about it and compared notes. That, I think, was a lovely route into writing because – and remember Finlay's insistence that limits create possibilities – I thought about ways of seeing and ideas of writing stories from different angles. Does this make sense to you?

I have been stronger lately and yesterday, for you, I was out and about for a little over half the day. I had shopping to do, but I deliberately extended it in increments in order to notice people and think about it all more, in the ways I have been suggesting in earlier chapters. I went into aisles in a supermarket where I needed nothing just to see what I would see.

What I saw was a nun buying mini eggs.

Ask and the universe answers. Ask and the book opens on the right page.

I do not believe in schmancy things like luck and magic because I'm a High-Church Anglo-Catholic, but then again, incredible things happen when you need a story.

Anyway, as I was saying:

I parked a way from a shop I needed to go to and walked down some little footpaths, alleyways, through the town; nothing overly beautiful, you understand, but practical municipal routes. I happened upon two young people apparently being cautioned by three police officers. Unsure how to navigate my way around this situation in physical terms, I made an awkward greeting with my hand half-raised and said hello in a quiet way.

As I emerged from this little footpath, I saw a man driving a tractor along the road near the centre of town. He was flamboyantly incongruous. The man – you would call him a gentleman farmer, I suppose – had a bespoke vintage tractor, which had been resprayed in silver. He was wearing a suit, and the tractor had an immaculate trailer on the back. Afterwards I wondered if I had seen it right – more on which in a moment.

On the last lap of this town walk, I passed a funeral director and watched a David Hasselhoff look-alike drive up in a private ambulance. He got up and walked to the doors at the back, and I knew (forgive me) he was about to bring a body into the premises. On the way, though, moving with quite impressive jollity and elan, he saw me and winked.

Driving home later on, I saw the same three police officers with, I thought, one of the

young people they had been with, plus someone else outside a house. Those two people were as far away as it would be possible to be in one space. It was the gap I noticed.

What would you have seen, though, if you had been on this journey or these walks for me? And what would I have imagined? To think of the difference is so exciting, and the thought and the distinct perspective can start from the most ordinary things, which we will come back to in the exercises at the end of this chapter.

There is something else I do to brings things alive and then make them better. Now Linn Webb, my editor at Bluemoose for my 2020 novel, *Saving Lucia*,[14] counsels writers to always read their work aloud. This is because you can then hear and feel the rhythm and cadence of your work and be aware of pace; also, you are better shown what works and what does not, where the pace stalls. (And it helps in spotting the inevitable typos, as it turns out!) In short, you are brought closer to what your reader reads and hears when they are engaging with the text for the first time. There is always a gap between you and your reader, and you have to try and take yourself closer to their experience for this to work. You do not have to be saying the words aloud, because you can feel it just by mouthing it. Give it a whirl.

But what has this excellent writing tip to do with walking and gentle productivity? Well, I found it productive to be reading my work aloud while moving – not going for a walk exactly, but moving about my home. Use an outside space if you have one. I found – does this sound too peculiar to you? – that moving while reading aloud helped me better to anchor the text and feel what was wrong, and I noticed that my movement stalled when the text did, or when there were clunky bits which I had not fully felt in reading them on a page. Now, this is only one perspective, and a quirky one, and not everyone is going to be able to do it, but why not try if it's an option?

As an alternative, one of my creative-writing students meets with a friend every Saturday morning – she is on the second draft of her novel – and her friend reads it aloud. They do a chapter every week – more if the mood takes them. Then, they *both* comment on what they noticed.

---

14 *Saving Lucia* (Hebden Bridge: Bluemoose Books, 2020). Also published as *Bang Bang Mussolini* (Milan: 8tto Edizione, 2023).

A key point I want to emphasise – and I will do so again after the exercises – is that some things do not feel like work but *are*. If you are writing a novel, a novella or a book of short stories, you might begin with a scene – or perhaps even smaller. There's a brilliant interview with the novelist Michael Ondaatje, partially reprinted in *The Kaizen Way*,[15] in which the novelist explains that he begins by posing small questions as he starts out on a book. This seemed a hugely doable thing to me – and you could use a walk to make observations which offer the food for these small questions, or to mull it all over once you have started. Truly, this is how I have written all my books and how I am making more. Back to the Ondaatje: he tells us he doesn't yet have any grand themes in his head, but rather a scattering of small incidents, rather than any intimidating grand questions. Setting out to make a book that is fascinating to readers would, for me, fire up anxiety and stymie creativity and any kind of productivity at all. But how about the scattering of incidents? It is refreshing and doable. He explains how he takes the idea of a plane crash or the idea of a patient and a nurse at night talking, and from there it is a simple navigation to more text: he might ask about the identity of the man in the plane; why is he there and what year is this? Asking questions is wonderfully fertile and little fragments, add up, so that you start finding out the past of these characters and about who they are. I want to add, however, once they start existing, one of the most exciting things in writing has already begun to happen: the characters turn up and do whatever they want and you need to get out of the way! Be flexible and enjoy the adventure.

---

15 Robert Maurer, *One Small Step Can Change Your Life: The Kaizen Way* (Bhopal: Manjul Publishing House, 2004), pp. 54–55.

An Exercise

(should I say *exercises*)

Go for a walk. OR, if you prefer, or if it's what you can do, go for a walk in your head.

First of all, try and *see* the characters I encountered. As you go, remember the Ondaatje ideas above, and ask small questions of the things you see. And keep it small, because small is a key element of gentle productivity in your writing, and trying to think about or make too much too soon might fire up anxiety or stop the task feeling doable.

The nun buying mini eggs: she had gleaming eyes. What was her backstory? Ought she to have been there? Why not? Why did you find this incongruous? What is her relationship with the other nuns? (Confession − *ho ho!* See what I did there? − I am really fascinated by nuns and monks, especially those in closed orders and − this is a story for another story − I do know and go to visit a group of Benedictine monks and have had to sit on my hands so that I don't write a book about them.)

The gentleman farmer: why was he dressed so smartly, and why the bespoke silver tractor? He was jaunty, and perhaps slightly haughty looking. Can you see him as you pass him? Is he a farmer at all, or is he really the chauffeur for a Wednesday wedding (this is not a particular thing − it just happened to be mid-week.) What if he is the groom − who is he marrying? Or is he escaping? Take him and his story in any direction you like.

The David Hasselhoff private ambulance driver is, to me, the most interesting of the characters I saw. He had an eighties beach glamour. Perhaps the other driver looks like Pamela Anderson (younger readers, please do look up the original *Baywatch* to know what on earth I am referring to). As with so much interest in life, the central point, the most piquant bit, is the incongruity. He is there with his private ambulance, and he spends his day doing this. Now, as a Celt I am naturally both morbid and open in my conversations about mortality, so I immediately started wondering if he talks to his charges. And why did he choose this career with his 80s California beach vibe? And when he winked was it because he liked the look of me or because he was meaning, 'So go we all' as he got ready to discharge his company to the funeral directors?

So much detail. Walk past him again. Perhaps in the other direction. Does he wink again, jovial and flirtatious, or has his look shifted? Does he now inhabit a different place as he goes about his work and his duty of care?

As for what appeared to be a cautioning by the police, my points of interest here, walking past and then reflecting on what I had briefly engaged with, in however superficial a way, were first that, by one action a life turns and alters radically – by one event, one wrong choice. The other point is that of social awkwardness in the way I met this gathering head-on and everyone looked at me. What do you see? What do you choose to focus on?

I could write a book of short stories based on all these encounters, and so could you. It might help to have a theme. Is it streets? Random encounters? Contrasts? Faiths? Turning points in lives – or the very incongruity of so many things we see? Such rich material!

That thought about, try these:

Go for a walk – literally or in your mind, by sinking into your imagination – and see things as if for the first time. *Really* look at them, whether it is the detail of lichen and moss on a wall, or the unfurling of a flower. Whether you are looking at the fonts in shop fronts or architectural detail – especially that which is unexpected – there is much new to see, if only new because you are only seeing it properly for the first time. Now look for small fragments – with people as well as physical objects: who made them and why? Trust that things and ideas will come to you. I hope that this will be helpful if you are just starting out on a book or if you are stuck. Or you have published one or more books and the new one won't come. To which I say, go into yourself, rest in the moment, as they say in meditation,[16] relax, then look out and think small.

On the same walk, or a different one, focus hard on your senses, including the shifting sensations under your feet. Also, consider your proprioception. That is, your perception and awareness of the movement of your body and your body in the space you are in. Skip this one if need be – and I have to say this is one I personally struggle with. Consider how it feels and what you feel if you can, though. All those things: what do you learn?

If you have a manuscript partly or fully written, record yourself reading the first section, or perhaps a piece that

16 I have found meditation life changing. Learning to relax has liberated me and keeping the focus on the present moment has dimmed my anxiety, helped me better understand rest, and meant that I could work more effectively in smaller increments. I do not say this lightly. I have had colossal stress in my life and over long periods. I love the Calmer app – at the time of writing, there was a version of the app you could have for free, but it's £39 for a year for all its resources.

has been problematic for you. Listen to it on your walk and feel its rhythm. What is wrong and what is right? Ponder it. Just listening to this as you tramp (or amble, or however you go) will help you not only to think about the section you have recorded, but about the whole book. You can get a tremendous amount of work done on a twenty-minute walk and listen. I know it's counter-intuitive, but productivity need not make you the whipping boy. It doesn't have to be all-in: you can be productive through a quiet engagement. In fact, I think it must be this way.

A general note of encouragement: much imaginative and intellectual grappling is solved by movement or the envisioning of movement – of activity. Have faith – in yourself, and in the world, which is full of detail and fascination.

When I talk to writers, I often find that they feel stymied because they think they do not have enough interest or dynamism in their lives to write a book drawing on their own lives, but I want to reassure you that this is not true, and we need to get past it. Gently making observations on ordinary things gives you a wealth of material, and it does not even feel like you are working.

But you ARE.

Chapter Six

On Creativity and Deep Sadness

A hand-holding essay.

I have written before about how writing need not be done in ideal conditions. If you wait for the planets to align, a better desk, a writing shed, more time, more supportive people about you or any number of other things, you may never start. You are, in effect, deferring your creativity to fate. To random acts. To heartbreak being mended.

But sometimes heartbreak is not mended.

I have a broken heart, and I have gradually come to the realisation that I have no sense of whether it will ever be mended.

I know that sounds bleak. But some problems do not have a solution; some things are not recoverable. There aren't always resources; there isn't always the will to help you; and illness or pain may not be fixable. Things do not always happen for a reason, and no, you are not only given what you can cope with – these are trite, empty affirmations, arid lies. *Of course they are.*

This is where I am right now.

But take my hand. Sometimes, as I sit at my desk, or the kitchen table, I can feel a deep pain in the region of my heart. This is not all, though. Yes, I sit there and feel it could be torn in two – 'break, heart, I prithee, break' – but it does not. It refuses.

Instead, here is what happens. I use words and small questions. I start asking myself those questions: How does it feel? What is happening elsewhere? Who can I hear? Somehow, those simple acts – focusing and using language to mould my experiences of the world – in the smallest viable way, right then, enable me to cope. Some say I am thriving. It is the greatest paradox, and is exactly what I want to reiterate about writing – both starting it or continuing.

You may think you are too put upon, ill or sad to ask those small questions and consider language and its aspirations: what it might do for you. This is not so. Sometimes, there is no happiness; you do not have that. In my case, there is the work. I teach teenagers, I mentor young adults and, increasingly, I am a creative-writing teacher too. There are my books. Everything you can read of mine has been forced on to the page, in small questions and small but resolute conversations with language. I have written sitting on the bonnet of my car in hospital car parks, lying on the floor at night on duty; I have reimagined what writing is, by coming fully to understand that it is not only setting the words on the page, but also thinking and reading. And as I said, that creative work, if you can trust just enough, will still emerge in the most disconsolate moods and times: even in a life which has come unstuck because of grief. Your intellect wants to play, to dance. Respond to it.

I know this piece is sad – and yet it is also not. At the heart of sadness is miracle. It does not fix anything, but it is still there, like an impulse to life. Perhaps it is not hope, but beauty.

You can trust me on this.

With all my love,

Anna

There is no exercise at the end of that chapter. Instead, I just want you to go and rest, lying down and closing your eyes if you like, and dream of stories. Or read aloud to yourself. How does that sound?

Chapter Seven

Doing Your Book in a Bubble Bath

The power of relaxation and rumination.
Because forgive me, productivity
need not only use your hands.

A short and restful chapter, this one.

Ah, relaxation. It is not what I am best at. To be frank, I am writing this book partly because I need to remind myself of what works best and what is good for me, as well as the process by which I feel writing a book becomes doable. Intrinsic to that is a quality of relaxation, and of joy, as I work. As you may have surmised, because you are both clever and intuitive, I am writing this book partly because it was the book – the companion – I needed. For me, it is not the writing itself which causes me trouble, but where it intersects with periods of feeling unwell and problems with the publishing industry – both of those have sub-categories, of course.

Let me make a bold suggestion. If there is a voice in your head saying you cannot structure a better sentence, ought not to be writing a book, people won't like you, or bad industry experience (we extrapolate and see patterns when anxious and low, I think) means that our experience will always be bad, and that is just what will happen to us, ad nauseam... Stop right there.

I expect that this is not your voice, but an embolism of received opinion and, as such, you might politely ask it to leave. Again.

Then, think about how you can relax more. For me, it is usually a combination of the outdoor world, nature, reading and being less in my head and more in my body. *Move freely within your own confinements*, for this could be a good thing. A little break will do you the world of good, and if you can do some stretches, or just be outside with the elements on your face, perhaps you will feel smaller – in a good way; perspective restored by this vast and gorgeous world – and, with that, so will negative feelings about writing and getting on with your book. This may feel like a time when you ought not to be away from your book, but this is not the case. When you are twitchy, restless, worrying, that is the very best time to be away. I've learned that the hard way, through pushing myself when I was tired because I foolishly said to myself that I ought to be able to do it! So many pals in the chronic illness and disability communities have set me on the right path with this one, understanding ways to manage rest, even in small increments. I found that, by doing less more, I did not sit idle; my work did not languish: no, instead I became more productive. Not necessarily rolling out more, but rolling out better.

An Exercise

Have a bubble bath. A few oils, if you like. My poisons of choice to drop in the bath are lavender, patchouli and geranium. I have been using oils since my mid-teens, and have always loved them. Try. You could make yourself a blend, as a signal: take time out from your book for a bubble bath plus these oils, or rub them on your hands, cup your hands and inhale. However you like.

Or, lie down, stretch, or just feel the sun, wind or damp (I am writing this in the UK, after all) on your face and know that you are powerfully alive. You are just plain old you – oh, but you are magnificent. HOORAY!

Then, give yourself over to daydreaming and loosely associative thought. Now, you could just see what happens, but I find that, if I've been feeling anxious, my mind fills with anxious thoughts. Don't try to banish them, but set another train of thought alongside. I play a game here. I say, 'I wonder... what if...' and I take a character, or place, or event, or feeling, from my writing, and I ask questions about it. 'I wonder... what if these two people had a conversation... fell in love... fell into bed when they should have been on the school run... what then? What happened, and how did it feel?' Let your mind wander: 'I wonder... what if the place I made had never existed or existed in the real world... who would miss it... what might it be replaced with... what was here first?'

Are you getting the hang of this? You are in the zone; you're in your book, *but* you're also taking yourself to one side of it and revelling in some restful adventures.

Here is the best bit, though: you get to relax and treat yourself well and let yourself off, AND YET you might have

71

unlocked something, solved something, done all kinds. And that is what I mean about gentle productivity: it comes in many forms, and it needs licence and for you to be playful.

Have faith.

I invite you to have a rest. I want you to go and sit quietly, somewhere where you won't (hopefully!) be disturbed. It may seem trite – embarrassing, even – but will you reflect at this point on the way in which you might use *The Alchemy*? Alternatively, just spend ten minutes or so saying some good stuff to yourself about yourself. It is not arrogant; it is careful and necessary self-regard. If you have written before, please remember to congratulate yourself on how far you have come.

Chapter Eight

Starter Sentences, Guided Reading Passages,

First Lines and HOT Questions

Do these help?

I believe that reading is our best teacher, so in this chapter, which is a little more technical but still, of course, gentle, I want us to look at these first lines of well-known novels and a story, and then at some longer sections of others. This chapter could be referred to at any stage of your book; use it to stimulate and focus thought, think about how interest is created in little language (opening lines), and how it is developed in longer first sections: how are you hooked and drawn in? I suggest you get into the habit of doing something like this regularly, plucking a book from your bookshelf (or wherever you keep your books) and asking yourself questions about how it's crafted, what is interesting for you; and, as well as thinking about what pulls you in, you could think about what pushes you out – in short, what don't you like? Little increments like this when you practise critical reading can be helpful for the development of your writing – in ideas, but also in looking at the way sentences are structured and, perhaps – look at number five below – how structures are subverted. You are building skill.[17] After all, go and look at *Finnegans Wake* by James Joyce, a book to which I am indebted: he can write like this (I am not budging) because he could craft a gorgeous but conservative sentence too; Picasso could master the abstract and the rebellious because he was also a master of ordinary (ordinary!) form – go and look up his drawings![18]

Call me Ishmael.

Herman Melville, Moby Dick, 1851

It was, as far as I can ascertain, in September of the year 1811 that a post-chaise drew up before the door of Aswarby Hall, in the heart of Lincolnshire. The little boy, who was the only passenger in the chaise, and who jumped out as soon as it had stopped, looked about him with the keenest curiosity during the short interval that elapsed between the ringing of the bell and the opening of the hall door.

M.R. James, Lost Hearts, 1895

---

17 For advice on close reading, I adore and really rate *Reading Like a Writer* – I have mentioned it before – by Francine Prose, and the follow-up, *What to Read and Why* (New York: Harper Collins, 2018).

18 I have taken older public-domain texts for copyright reasons and thought I would use this opportunity to tell you about Project Gutenberg – the vast and brilliant free library of texts that are out of copyright. Go and explore: it will change your life; but do leave a donation every now and then? https://www.gutenberg.org/

It was the best of times, it was the worst of times, it was the age of wisdom, it was the age of foolishness, it was the epoch of belief, it was the epoch of incredulity, it was the season of Light, it was the season of Darkness, it was the spring of hope, it was the winter of despair, we had everything before us, we had nothing before us, we were all going direct to heaven, we were all going direct the other way – in short, the period was so far like the present period that some of its noisiest authorities insisted on its being received, for good or for evil, in the superlative degree of comparison only.

Charles Dickens, *A Tale of Two Cities*, 1859

My true name is so well known in the records or registers at Newgate, and in the Old Bailey, and there are some things of such consequence still depending there, relating to my particular conduct, that it is not be expected I should set my name or the account of my family to this work; perhaps, after my death, it may be better known; at present it would not be proper, no not though a general pardon should be issued, even without exceptions and reserve of persons or crimes.

Daniel Defoe, *Moll Flanders*, 1722

And here is one from me!

Violet Albina Gibson, the Honourable, was behind bars, wearing an immaculate black crêpe dress, clasping her finest manners and a lovely, lacquered fountain pen, for letters to Churchill and others.

Anna Vaught, *Saving Lucia*, 2020

When you read these, ask yourself the broad questions: what do you think, what do you like, how do you feel? What on earth is going on? What does it remind you of? Feel free to add any questions of your own.

Next, here are the beginnings of three very well-known books, and after each, I have offered you some questions. I like to teach creative writing using a lot of close reading (and I read closely for my own writing), so that is what I encourage you to do here – this time, in looking at how character and landscape are developing, think about how you are hooked, how contrasts are used and, indeed, where beguiling ambiguities are deployed. Notice situational details and how these provide texture and interest, as well as contextualising characters and giving you clues to their personalities and psychologies. When you're answering the questions, don't think of there being a right answer: this is not a test! I'm just encouraging you to observe closely, ponder and of course enjoy what you're reading. Relax while you do this – perhaps reading the sections aloud, if you can, and, as you go, let a question settle in: *How might what I find here help in my writing?*

Great Expectations

Charles Dickens, 1860

MY FATHER'S FAMILY NAME being Pirrip, and my Christian name Philip, my infant tongue could make of both names nothing longer or more explicit than Pip. So, I called myself Pip, and came to be called Pip.

I give Pirrip as my father's family name, on the authority of his tombstone and my sister – Mrs Joe Gargery, who married the blacksmith. As I never saw my father or my mother, and never saw any likeness of either of them (for their days were long before the days of photographs), my first fancies regarding what they were like were unreasonably derived from their tombstones. The shape of the letters on my father's gave me an odd idea that he was a square, stout, dark man, with curly black hair. From the character and turn of the inscription, '*Also Georgiana Wife of the Above*', I drew a childish conclusion that my mother was freckled and sickly. To five little stone lozenges, each about a foot and a half long, which were arranged in a neat row beside their grave, and were sacred to the memory of five little brothers of mine – who gave up trying to get a living, exceedingly early in that universal struggle – I am indebted for a belief I religiously entertained that they had all been born on their backs with their hands in their trousers' pockets, and had never taken them out in this state of existence.

Ours was the marsh country, down by the river, within, as the river wound, twenty miles of the sea. My first most vivid and broad impression of the identity of things seems to me to have been gained on a memorable raw afternoon towards evening. At such a time I found out for certain that this bleak place overgrown with nettles was the churchyard; and that Philip Pirrip, late of this parish, and also Georgiana wife of the above, were dead and buried; and that Alexander, Bartholomew, Abraham, Tobias and Roger, infant children of the aforesaid, were also dead and buried; and that the dark flat wilderness beyond the churchyard, intersected with dykes and mounds and gates, with scattered cattle feeding on it, was

77

the marshes; and that the low leaden line beyond was the river; and that the distant savage lair from which the wind was rushing was the sea; and that the small bundle of shivers growing afraid of it all and beginning to cry, was Pip.

Questions

1. What do we find out about Pip, and how is it communicated to you?
2. What is the impact, for you, of the first-person address?
3. How do you think the evocative description of landscape feeds into your appreciation of who and what Pip is?
4. The gravestones: there are no photographs; Pip must see his parents and his siblings by reading the stones. Think about it: when you started writing your book, or as you begin now, did you, too, start imagining characteristics, traits and physiognomies, too? Were they the same as Pip's?

The Great Gatsby

F. Scott Fitzgerald, 1925

I N MY YOUNGER and more vulnerable years my father gave me some advice that I've been turning over in my mind ever since.

'Whenever you feel like criticising anyone,' he told me, 'just remember that all the people in this world haven't had the advantages that you've had.'

He didn't say any more, but we've always been unusually communicative in a reserved way, and I understood that he meant a great deal more than that. In consequence, I'm inclined to reserve all judgements, a habit that has opened up many curious natures to me and also made me the victim of not a few veteran bores. The abnormal mind is quick to detect and attach itself to this quality when it appears in a normal person, and so it came about that in college I was unjustly accused of being a politician, because I was privy to the secret griefs of wild, unknown men. Most of the confidences were unsought – frequently I have feigned sleep, preoccupation or a hostile levity when I realised by some unmistakable sign that an intimate revelation was quivering on the horizon; for the intimate revelations of young men, or at least the terms in which they express them, are usually plagiaristic and marred by obvious suppressions. Reserving judgements is a matter of infinite hope. I am still a little afraid of missing something if I forget that, as my father snobbishly suggested, and I snobbishly repeat, a sense of the fundamental decencies is parcelled out unequally at birth.

And, after boasting this way of my tolerance, I come to the admission that it has a limit. Conduct may be founded on the hard rock or the wet marshes, but after a certain point I don't care what it's founded on. When I came back from the East last autumn, I felt that I wanted the world to be in uniform and at a sort of moral attention for ever; I wanted no more riotous excursions with privileged glimpses into the human heart. Only Gatsby, the man who gives his name to this book, was exempt from my reaction – Gatsby, who represented everything for which I have an unaffected scorn. If personality is an unbroken series of successful gestures, then there was something gorgeous about him, some heightened sensitivity to the promises of life, as if he were related to one of those intricate machines that register earthquakes ten thousand miles away. This responsiveness had nothing to do with that flabby impressionability which is dignified under the name of the 'creative temperament' – it was an extraordinary gift for hope, a romantic readiness such as I have never found in any other person and which it is not likely I shall ever find again. No – Gatsby turned out all right at the end; it is what preyed on Gatsby, what foul dust floated in the wake of his dreams that temporarily closed out my interest in the abortive sorrows and short-winded elations of men.

Questions

1. The narrator is Nick. Reading through these first paragraphs, do you trust him? If not, why? If you do trust him, are you unsettled at all?

2. What do you think has been set up in terms of contrast, difference, between the narrator and the world of Gatsby?

3. Can you analyse how this hooks you – or tries to! – in terms of how the character is introduced?

4. What impact do the things which 'preyed' and the 'foul dust' have on your impression of both Nick and Gatsby, whom we have yet to meet, though he seems to be established as the main character...

Middlemarch

George Eliot, 1871

'Since I can do no good because a woman,
Reach constantly at something that is near it.'
            – The Maid's Tragedy,
            BEAUMONT AND FLETCHER

MISS BROOKE HAD THAT kind of beauty which seems to be thrown into relief by poor dress. Her hand and wrist were so finely formed that she could wear sleeves not less bare of style than those in which the Blessed Virgin appeared to Italian painters; and her profile as well as her stature and bearing seemed to gain the more dignity from her plain garments, which by the side of provincial fashion gave her the impressiveness of a fine quotation from the Bible – or from one of our elder poets – in a paragraph of today's newspaper. She was usually spoken of as being remarkably clever, but with the addition that her sister Celia had more common sense. Nevertheless, Celia wore scarcely more trimmings; and it was only to close observers that her dress differed from her sister's, and had a shade of coquetry in its arrangements; for Miss Brooke's plain dressing was due to mixed conditions, in most of which her sister shared. The pride of being ladies had something to do with it: the Brooke connections, though not exactly aristocratic, were unquestionably 'good': if you inquired backward for a generation or two, you would not find any yard-measuring or parcel-tying forefathers – anything lower than an admiral or a clergyman; and there was even an ancestor discernible as a Puritan gentleman who served under Cromwell, but afterwards conformed, and managed to come out of all political troubles as the proprietor of a respectable family estate. Young women of such birth, living in a quiet country house, and attending a village church hardly larger than a parlour, naturally regarded frippery as the ambition of a huckster's daughter. Then there was well-bred economy, which in those days made show in dress the first item to be deducted from, when any margin was required for expenses more distinctive of rank. Such reasons would have been enough to account for plain dress, quite apart from religious feeling; but in Miss Brooke's case, religion alone would have determined it; and Celia mildly acquiesced in all her sister's sentiments, only infusing them with that common sense which is able to accept momentous doctrines without any eccentric agitation. Dorothea knew many passages of Pascal's *Pensées* and of Jeremy Taylor by heart; and to her the destinies of mankind, seen by the light of Christianity, made the solicitudes of feminine fashion appear an occupation for Bedlam. She could not reconcile the anxieties of a spiritual life involving eternal consequences, with a keen interest in gimp and artificial protrusions of drapery. Her mind was theoretic, and yearned by its nature after some lofty conception of the world which might frankly include the parish of Tipton and her own rule of conduct there; she was enamoured of intensity and greatness, and rash in embracing whatever seemed to her to have those aspects; likely to seek martyrdom, to make retractations and then to incur martyrdom after all in a quarter where she had not sought it. Certainly such elements in the character of a marriageable girl tended to interfere with her lot, and hinder it from being decided according to custom, by good looks, vanity and merely canine affection. With all this, she, the elder of the sisters, was not yet twenty, and they had both been educated, since they were about twelve years old and had lost their parents, on plans at once narrow and promiscuous, first in an English family and afterwards in a Swiss family at Lausanne, their bachelor uncle and guardian trying in this way to remedy the disadvantages of their orphaned condition.

Questions

1. What clues does the epigraph give to the characters we are about to meet?
2. What are the subtle contrasts set up between Celia and her sister Dorothea?
3. How are objects used to suggest character – such as clothing and jewellery?
4. This is trickier: what is the tone of the narrative regarding either or both two women? To put it another way, what is the writer's attitude towards their subject matter as shown by their expression here?

Next, here are some starter suggestions on character and a few things to get you thinking – and you can be thinking about these at any time at all. The key thing is ASKING AND RESPONDING TO QUESTIONS. Asking questions is key to writing your book. If you are part of a writing group, or have a trusted friend who's also writing, or interested in it, you might do this together. Important. People will have varied responses to these – do not be startled if someone's thoughts are radically different from yours or if either of you find these questions hard. I have formed these specifically to focus on character, and as such you can use them both when starting to write a book and when you are underway, developing and rounding out your characters. It's a way of really thinking about who they are, feeling them – having them at your table, as I like to say. Some of these may sound odd, but bear with me. Each thought ladders, you see: it leads you on to deep and interesting questions about a character.

1. What kind of music does your character like, and why is that?
2. How do they react to temperatures and to weather?
3. Can they tell a funny joke?
4. If you asked them do describe it, what might have been a key formative experience for them – in childhood, for example?
5. Do they dress colourfully, or blend in as much as possible with muted colours? Why might that be? Or are they indifferent to their appearance, in fact?
6. Solitary or social? Choice or circumstance? Ponder that and what it has to do with character, remembering that character is both inherent and built from layers of experience...
7. What are their political beliefs? Or do they think that politics has nothing to do with them?
8. Have they ever been in love?
9. What are the most important things in their lives?
10. What is their attitude to time? Are they inclined to live in the past, or in anxiety, say, about the future, or are they grounded in the moment?

I should add that any or all of these might also be useful for a single short story or short-fiction collection, as well as creative non-fiction and memoir – in which case, ask these questions of yourself; just change the pronouns as you go. Tell you what: it could be that this set of exercises sparks a whole new book, story, or idea for a project – so do share what happens!

Chapter Nine

Journeying and Writing

When you are on the move, whether from room to room
or on your way to New York. Or Slough,
Cwmbran or Wigan.

You will by now have noticed that central to this book is the idea of careful, relaxed, intricate observation. I do not assume that readers of this book on writing will be able to travel, that they do a commute, that they do other than remain housebound. In our lives and imaginations, as I am at pains to communicate, there are riches, and the life that is constrained by illness, funds or confidence is not less rich intellectually. I see tweets and pieces of writing about how a good writer needs to have a rich life, full of varied experience, and I have strong feelings about this.

Oh yeah?

Yeah. That is an immensely privileged and ableist thing to say.

Actually, I feel a bit cross that it gets said.

So bollocks to it.

You go where you go and where you can go, my darling.

So let's spend some time on actual journeys – on those which seem the least promising in terms of what they might offer a creator (not so), but also on imaginary journeys, or even a traverse of the room we are in, because this is all about seeing and noticing. Most of all, though, we need to remember that the quality to focus on is not the experience, but the reaction to it; that is, the energy and depth of thoughts. The bulk of writing, as I have said before, is in thinking.

I am quite taken with a notion from the French painter, soldier and writer, Xavier de Maistre, 1763–1852. In his 1794 book *A Journey Around My Room*,[19] he describes how, when confined to his home in Turin as a consequence of a duel, he would explore the room travelling, making sense of space. He even wrote a sequel where he ventured out on to his balcony at night because his brother was so enthused by the text.

Now, de Maistre had a valet and backup – let's not compare his aristocratic life with ours; and remember, also, that the book is a parody, and Xavier did not think much of it; in fact, the book only came to publication because his brother, Joseph de Maistre, did value the book. However, I have enjoyed the imagination of this book – the way this mock travelogue plays with perception and our sense of what is valuable and of interest; it is also, for me – and perhaps for you too – a reminder to observe intently, an indication that

19 Xavier de Maistre, *A Journey Around My Room* (originally published in French as *Voyage autour de ma chambre* in 1794), trans. Henry Attwell (London: Longmans, Green, Reader and Dyer, 1871).

one can journey across a room just as well as to Lucknow, or Ottawa, or Cwmbran – or maybe even Didcot (where there is fascination, but that is a story for another day)!

De Maistre writes:

My room is situated in latitude 48° east, according to the measurement of Father Beccaria. It lies east and west, and, if you keep very close to the wall, forms a parallelogram of thirty-six steps round. My journey will, however, be longer than this; for I shall traverse my room up and down and across, without rule or plan.

And:

Upon opening the first drawer to the left, we find an inkstand, paper of all kinds, pens ready mended and sealing wax; all which set the most indolent person longing to write.

How would it be if, looking around the room you are in, you situated yourself geographically and looked at where you were on the map? Find yourself on Google Maps, or pull out an old Ordnance Survey, whatever you like. Zoom in and out. What happens to your perceptions and feelings when you do that, imagining how very tiny you are on that tiny journey you just made with a slight drift of a mouse, brush of a thumb on a screen or rustle of pages. And I wonder: did it make you think in an unusual way about someone or something you are trying to write about, or maybe an aspect of their response, or where they were in relation to the world? Not just geographically, but in inter-relational terms, or spiritual?

Look back in and really come into the room, noting all that is in it. Take a journey, like de Maistre, traversing – which could just be in thought, as your eyes proceed to note what is there and really see it. I had better explain that, and I will move around the room I am now, in real time, with spontaneous results just for you. When I am looking, I am also letting my imagination freewheel, and I indulge it, if thoughts, associations or memories come to me. The first thing I see is what's right in front of me: a big pot of felt-tips and coloured pencils. Observing this in detail, I am enjoying the assorted colours, noting that many of them are the same brand; I enjoy the continuity. Now I notice that there are five pens from a different packet, and I start asking myself questions: why is that? Where are the rest – and who has them? Now I see that the bulk have a smooth tip, and five have a ridged, variegated lid, and so I wonder about the provenance of that design and the justification for it. What taste lay there, at some point, and was there an emotion behind it? What about the decision to use a serif font rather sans serif for the 'felt-tip pens' lettering on the side of each pen? Then, in gold, giving a hint of opulence. Can, I think, a felt-tip pen ever be opulent? Did the designer or whoever was in charge of branding have a sense of humour? I am asking myself questions about all these things, and my eyes travel up, because I am front of a window, and I can see a neighbouring garden: twice a day they come to feed the birds – you can set your watch by it; and it's not all birds but a large collection of rooks, who croak and perform that strange gargle they have. And I love a rook, a corvid – crows and ravens, too. They are clever, and behind Paddington station there is a talking raven. Or was. Did you know that? You do now. I might look at a whole garden or I might cover twenty square centimetres, and find riches on my travels, just by letting my thought go, allowing associations to form freely and, moreover, by asking questions.

This is vital – and if you were wondering where on earth I was going with this chapter, it was with questions. On your room-travel, leave no stone unturned. If an object does nothing for you, move straight on, but keep asking questions; questions are the strong lines of your book. Questions are the things which pull a reader with us through our book.[20] In some genres of books – say, psychological thrillers or mystery stories – the question is asked loudly; whereas in others the question may be much quieter – but that is not to say that it is less powerful. Getting into the habit of asking questions right where you are – yes, even you are channelling Xavier de Maistre and traversing your room – will help you practise that. I would argue that is a natural human instinct to want to complete missing information, but it can be honed further by being more inquisitive on the smallest journeys.

You will have a huge degree of options if you are on a bus, in a crowded station (I realise I might be romanticising this, because, as I look at the news now, in January 2023, I know I would be tearing my hair out if I were in the current chaos at London Bridge), but even then, look and spectate: notice behaviour, stance and interaction.

---

20 We have already met the idea of asking questions as you begin – or deepen – your book in chapter five.

Ask questions and remember your strong lines as you go.

Back to my view from the window and the corvids. Some of the neighbours behind our house tend not to speak to others in the area, and there has been some conflict. My question is: Why? What originates there, and is it pain? Then I see and hear the rooks being fed, and it is so close and tender – a conversation with nature. Remember I am looking at that twenty-centimetre-square prospect and I see love, clemency – a slow approach to the bird table and careful placing of bread and seeds on the bird table. My question is: Why is there a disparity between contacts here? And that broadens into questions I could ask about how suspicion of others – the other – begins; yet it softens in the natural world or in situations when the heart contracts with joy. That's both troubling and fascinating to me.

So, you see, you need not have a life full of travel and incident, because even in a small world there is fascinating detail to observe or expound upon. To share something from my own family: a much-loved relative has lived for seventy-five years, yet never been abroad and has rarely been beyond a small corner of south-west Wales. You might say, Look what they have missed! But consider it another way: think – just think – what they have seen.

It is the quality of thought and observation that makes the difference, and sometimes, referring to my relative again, it is counter-intuitive. The richest narrative, the most flexible and shifting thinking and the most radiant spirit in the family belongs to the person who has been to the fewest places and whose experience, if you had not been paying attention, is the most bounded. *It is the seeing eye and the dynamic mind.*

Be that person with your book and its questions – its strong lines – whether you are able to travel or must stay where you are.

Exercises

Spend ten minutes on these.

Sit down – or lie down – and take an area of your room and traverse it. You could move or just take a small view in front of you, as I described above. What is there, and how is it, as its meaning and layers unfold, in whatever way they do, a story? Or, how does anything you are meditating on link to something you have already written about in your book? Does it illuminate anything?

If you are out and about, perhaps on a train or bus, maybe on a plane, or a passenger in a car, keep a notebook with you and use these prompts.

Explore your senses...

Describe people...

Conversations...

Highs and lows...

What is the weather like?

...And finally – fuck it, I do this ALL THE TIME – who do I fancy here?

Chapter Ten

On Cheerful and Productive Failure

Nothing is new. Ever anything but. Everything attempted.
And no doubt failed. But not to worry. Try once more.
Fail once more. But fail better. On your arse.

(As Samuel Beckett almost wrote.)

That is Samuel Beckett. From his 1983 prose work, *Worstward
Ho*. OK, it's paraphrased, because otherwise permission fees
would set my eyes watering, but you get the gist. It is funny.
Recently, I have been wondering if it's the new 'Keep Calm
and Carry On' – in which case we could have a 'Fail Better'
gallery: mugs, doormats, handcuffs, you name it. What would
Beckett have thought? Probably that it was foolishness, but
hopefully he would have laughed.

I digress. Why do I begin with this quotation? My late
grandmother once said something along the lines of how you
had to fail with style and in an interesting way before you
could call yourself a grown-up. That stuck with me. She also
said that you have to get quickly up off your arse when the
devil vomits into your kettle, which was a terrifying jumble
of stuff. Could have been Beckett with a bit of polishing, my

slightly scary Welsh grandma. Anyway, I don't think she took the bit about failure far enough: I think you keep doing it. I'm not saying you actually aim for it, but that you accept it, more, as the natural state of things, just with economies of scale.

Now, I have failed aplenty. I like to recast it: so I failed majestically, heroically, as if I were looking at me from the wings, going, 'See what you did there?' (actually, I sort of did that: read my autobiographical novel, *Killing Hapless Ally*[21] for a load of that), and clapping like a pissed cheerleader. True, there have been some comical moments of failure: falling off a desk in front of a GCSE class and tearing down an entire wall display of their work in trying to steady myself; attending meetings with my dress tucked into my knickers; in another meeting accidentally saying 'sex' when I meant 'notes'; talking a bit too excitedly to mums on the school run and seeing them begin to sidle away; very recently saying to a class teacher, 'Has my son been a bit of a twat?' when I meant 'twit'; falling asleep on my first date with my husband and falling over in a perfectly flat field on my second. That sort of thing. I relate these sorts of things to others sometimes, should we be discussing delicious things like, I don't know, embarrassment, and it might happen that they go, 'Noooo… how awful' – and I think, 'Do you not do that sort of thing regularly too?' Then I think maybe it's just me, like a dervish at a particularly stifled funeral. But I'm not so sure. It's not that others will have done the same things, but, truly, everyday embarrassments and failures: aren't they normal? Human.

These are not important failures. Just an untidy life.

---

21 *Killing Hapless Ally* (Manningtree: Patrician Press, 2016).

There are bigger things too. Hearts I broke, people I disappointed. The fact that my mother thought I sucked. That my brother hated the fact that I was born. No point in not being frank at this juncture, I would say. Some of these things I thought to be my fault, but time and reflection may tell a different story. Ah, what else? Career blips – no career; the PhD I didn't complete (I won't tell you the whole story here); the fact that people weren't very nice to me on my wedding day (on reflection, this one might not be on me) – oooh, loads of stuff. Parenting mistakes; financial ones; soured relationships. Just get out of here! This is not very interesting. It's more that I want to tell you you're not alone. But most of the time, I, you, we did our best, yes? Then there you go.

You can get big, bold places, high on failure, and not seem to know it. Donald Trump was a colossal failure as a president. His world view is egregiously limited, his ego needing to be regularly stroked because it must be upheld, delicate as gossamer. Do you think he goes to bed worrying about his failure or reflecting on it? In the UK, what of Johnson? What of Truss? Sunak? Well, I haven't been with Donald at bedtime, praise the Lord, but I rather doubt it. And therein lies the crux of the matter: to acknowledge that you misjudge, misprise and misrule; to be compassionate and self-aware enough to know that you failed, and to attempt, where you can, to make amends – that is the key thing. When it's missing, what might that make you? Appetitive; governed by your own wants and a desire to be, err, stroked and told that you are right. Ugh. That makes me want to barf on my shoes – and oh, it makes me cross. I realise I am simplifying things about Trump, and that he probably has some latent virtues, but he seemed a decent enough exemplar.

To be human is to err. To err splendiferously. In teaching – and I don't know why anyone would pretend otherwise – you will misunderstand some of those you are teaching and fail to see their ability, their wants – even, sometimes, the terrible pain they might be in. You will get a lot right, but you will also get a lot wrong. In your life, you will accidentally upset friends; you will say things that reverberate in others' ears for an awfully long time. But you did your best, and that's all that can be asked of you. If it's a failure where you know you have hurt someone and done what you can to fix it and make amends, if you've felt guilt and reflected and looked at yourself sternly – painful but necessary – then take that and move forward – and not just for yourself. Learn. If it is a comical failure – like, say, trying a new sexual position (I actually had a conversation about this recently, which reduced me to helpless, snorty laughter and tears – and no, I am not naming its provenance), striking the bedside lamp in flagrante and singeing the side of the duvet, please LAUGH. You know what's not hot? Being joyless and mirthless. You know what's not sexy? Perfection. Also, it's bollocks – it doesn't exist.

I had a friend once (note past tense) who said, with passionate confidence, 'I don't know what failure is. I have never failed at anything.' I was in awe of her: I had chronically low self-esteem, was battling depression; I thought she was someone to look up to. How wrong was I? Humility and humour, kindness – that's where it's at. That is success. Arrogance is not success.[22] That

---

22 As I like to say to people when they share they have imposter syndrome, 'Better this than be an arrogant twat, because it's the arrogant twats who break things.'

is definitely a failure, in my book. Anyway, I don't see this person any more. I do not wish them ill – and they may be deliriously happy, for all I know, sharp-suited and driven... but maybe not having messy sex in the back of a pick-up, or feeding a sad-looking pony an apple, or even comforting another person whose life has unravelled at the seams. What do you think? Am I over-simplifying?

Parenting's a revelation for this success/failure malarkey. I have seen other parents chortle at how their child is top of the pecking order, or, say, without apology, announce that their child will go a long way and, in the mean time, tends only to be friends with other high-achievers. It is bang on to be proud of your child (I have three myself), but A) your child is not an extension through which (she says cattily) you get to swat drippy under-achieving fellow parents (like me), and B) can you HEAR YOURSELF? Pipe down.

So now, you see, we have ascertained that failure is normal. A lot of dreams and career aspirations tank. Of course they do. Marriages, or your final sense of acquiring a sense of identity may feel incomplete. In some work – in the creative industries – I would argue that failure is hardwired into your job. You'll have your work rejected – or not even acknowledged. But hey there, frownie, suck it up. It is normal. Fail once more, fail better. Continue. I do think – and I speak as someone who has had many years of battling mental-health problems – that we place too much emphasis on achievement. And not, I might say, always that achievement which is in line with our core values – with what we truly believe and value. If you are driven, then go drive, but maybe know that when you get to the place called THERE, you might well discover that there's no THERE there (if you follow my meaning). I am not suggesting that we don't aim for things we would like to do or be – just that it might be healthier and make us happier if we were honest about these things. And – I speak from hard-won experience here – I do not think it helps to be led by comparison with others. In fact, I'd say, 'compare and despair'. I know that when I do that, the comparison thing, I am inclined to come off worse and will likely feel awful, physically and mentally. I did kind of tell you at the beginning there that I was an epic failure!

There has been a great deal of study on this topic of late, so it might not be news to you that social media and what we absorb and ingest therein can be a problem. I talk to the teenagers I teach about it. Some of them struggle, but find they can't stay away, frightened to miss out. But that feeling is not unique to those in this demographic and, in fact, I'd argue that younger people are often way more sensible than older people, and not just because they are digital natives. But I think we all need to be mindful of the fact that what we see is a version of reality: a curated narrative. I love social media for the friends I've made and things I've been able to learn; the writing project I am currently pursuing came to me through Twitter. A picture, a conversation: serendipitous, exciting and joyful. But the braggy, showy stuff can go hang.

Is all this depressing? I would say no. Stuff up. Let go. Go and rehearse the facts of life in a sober manner, and I wonder if you might actually start to giggle. Because the failure provides a much better anecdote and releases you from much stress. Achieve, according to your own lights – but when I go, I just want to be remembered (if you do remember me) as the funny lady who tried every day to be kind. Fell on her arse constantly. Loved Jesus but enjoyed cursing. Embraced paradox and irreverence. And pie. And kittens. And gave a sad-looking pony an apple. You know.

> Nothing is new. Ever anything but. Everything attempted. And no doubt failed. But not to worry. Try once more. Fail once more. But fail better. On your arse.

Beckett was THE KING. Even in paraphrase.
> On you go, then. Humiliation is rarely fatal.
> Love, Anna

Rather than an exercise for this chapter, here's what I want you to do – and it is simple but powerful. Read something in a genre, form or about a topic which is not normally in your wheelhouse. See what happens. In other words, experiment with and broaden your reading. Do it now and keep it up. Incredible things can happen, you know.

Chapter Eleven

On Love and On What Love Is Not

This is a difficult chapter to write, and you may disagree with what I say, but if this chapter touches a heart, holds a hand and liberates someone, then its work is done: it need only be one. I will keep this brief, and anyway, many of its sentiments are echoed in other chapters and aim to provide you with easement and a sense of shared endeavour – with me, I mean! I will also explain what I mean by 'love' for the purposes of this chapter.

It may be that you struggled in school. I am a schoolteacher and a mentor for young people. I promise you that not everyone in a school knows what they are talking about – education is one thing, but we have to be sceptical about at least part of it, and teachers do not, with the best will in the world, leave their personalities, insecurities and bias at the door. So I would like you, first of all, to aim to break free a little from expectations. I will use myself as an example.

Other than my year-seven English teacher (when I was aged eleven to twelve), no one *ever* identified any creative-writing ability in me. I am not saying I am a genius of a writer – OF COURSE NOT – but I also know that creative writing was not promoted around me, and I felt my efforts were rebuffed. My advice to you would be to push forward, hopefully comforted by what I just told you. You have to develop a mixture of gentle self-belief and sheer bloody-mindedness, but you do not have to do it all at once. This is, after all, a book about gentle productivity, and that starts with one word at a time. Let me also hand you this card… right, got it – in fact, have two…

Restrictions: too old, wrong colour, wrong class, wrong gender. I hate all this. You carry it with you, like a stone in your heart. There is nothing wrong with you, *nothing less;* the problems stem from bias in others and, in some cases, from perceived bias. For you to move forward, it is essential to gather around you a small tribe of people whom you trust and who appreciate how you feel, so try to form a little writing group, carefully curated – it could be online. This in hand, I hope you feel a little more secure, and you can accept you do not need the approval of everyone – neither do you need permission from publishers or the perceived world out there to write a book. If you feel scared, I think you might be more likely to rush at the task in hand, which is something I know I have done. Instead, take your time to form a writing support group, and proceed gently, slowly, from there.

Self-talk: what about how you speak to yourself and what rattles around in your head? May I entertain you with a low-key rant? I know some people like an inspirational fridge magnet starring Maya Angelou (it bothers me that many readers only know Angelou as a fridge magnet, so I urge you to read her books, essays and poetry collections); others stick post-its with affirmations written on them on the bathroom mirror, to look at when they brush their teeth. *You are enough*, they say. *But what if you're not*, I think – there have been many times when I could try all I liked but my efforts and I were not enough. *Just one small positive thought in the morning can change your whole day* – but what if you cannot think of anything positive? And it's not going to do much good if calamity befalls you, or if a seagull shits massively on your head on the way to your dream job interview. *Opportunities don't happen, you create them.* This assumes there is no such thing as structural inequality. And of course there are the particularly awful, *It is never too late to be what you might have been* and *When you have a dream, you've got to grab it and never let go*. Well, plainly it sometimes is too late – sometimes that ship has sailed; and some dreams are evidently ridiculous – you're (probably) not currently starring in *Les Misérables*. As for the egregious quotation attributed to Audrey Hepburn, *Nothing is impossible. The word itself says, 'I'm possible'*, I'd posit this is plainly not true, because some things are impossible – and the word impossible does not contain 'I'm possible', for, as you know, because you're a writer, the word impossible does not contain an apostrophe and *im-* as a prefix is 'no' or 'not'. And I am fine with limits. Because you cannot do everything: this is not a cosmic catalogue from which we order, and apostrophes are our friends.

You MUST ignore me if you love these quotes, because I am speaking only of taste, which is always going to be subjective, relative, culture-bound, whether I can see it or not. However, I suggest a new mantra for when negative thoughts appear about writing and your ability to be – your right to be – a creator. My affirmation is *FUCK OFF*.

Yes, *fuck off* to all those pesky thoughts that say you can't be this, you are dim, didn't shine, cannot write because there is too much going on. If someone else said these things to someone you love, you would not tolerate it, so please don't do it to yourself. This is love – from you. Kindness (but not that nauseating hashtag which usually – in publishing, anyway – issues from people who are a bit wanky; apologies – I am quite fired up in this chapter): kindness to your sad self. Offer yourself reassurance, trust in your ideas and imagination and rational mind, and trust that you can make a book, or any other extended creative project, for that matter, in little steps and as, when and how your mind and body need.

What about the way others regard you – family responses, antipathy from friends? This is tricky, but first, you're on a hiding to nothing if you assume that understanding comes with love. Clearly that would be ideal, but I would argue that those who love you may be baffled by you. Human beings are baffling creatures – I do not understand myself all the time and keep bad faith sometimes because I am corrupt and broken, just like you are. If I don't understand myself, how on earth could I expect you to? I am encouraging you, then, not to insist to yourself that someone doesn't love you if they do not understand you. Letting go of this expectation is a liberating thing.

Then, consider that writing books is a slightly odd thing. Some people find it weird: you could just read them – there *are* already plenty of books! – and others think of writing only as a hobby, which does not incline them to take it as seriously as you. Again, let go; do not look for affirmation. I am giving it to you, and so are other writers. Remind yourself that it is important to you!

What, then, if family and friends criticise you or demean you for writing? I talk to people about this a great deal. There must be some complicated feelings about writing because, for many people, it is an aspirational thing. Writing a book is something that many aspire to – *there is a book in me,* you often hear – but if they have not started to write, it might piss them off they you have. I have even been asked, *Who do you think you are?* This is because some others regard the attainment or the journey towards attainment as pretentious or arrogant, as if books were not written by people from all walks of life and as if this had historically not been the case.

Let it go. No, what is said may not feel loving, but consider that humans are complicated, and pursuing a particular path may irritate others for reasons which have nothing to do with you. It can help to approach these clashes with compassion – but you do not have to take it on board.

To go back to the title of this chapter, 'On Love and On What Love Is Not', I would advise you to lower your standards, because you can still be loved if you and your work are not understood; love is a pure gift, and we cannot attach requirements to it like this. Then, someone can love you and say things that are unloving; and you must regard yourself with compassion, with love. If you constantly look for affirmation, look instead to your own self and what you think. YOU are the author. When you have done your book, with a bit of luck, you will be on your way to wonderful engagements with readers. They – mostly people you do not know and whom you will never meet – will have a life enhanced by something you made. THAT is a loving exchange.

For everything else, gaslighting, persistent criticism, do not turn to shallow affirmations, but remember *fuck off* and bear in mind the cards I made you. You needn't say these aloud or do something appalling like putting it repeatedly in a book, as I just did, but stick it around the house, on post-its, have a bangle made – whatever you like. Greet your work with the spirit of rebellion. I shall be so very proud of you.

Exercises

Are you a bit tired today? Let us keep this one simple.

1. You could download and print off the permission cards in this book from the Alchemy forum. Or get a sharpie and write the same things, defiantly, with a sure hand, on post-its or scraps of paper. Put them on the bathroom mirror or fridge – or everywhere! I want you to feel liberated and to know that someone understands that you can feel fragile, that you can feel an outsider. We are all outsiders.

2. Right now, note what you are proud of in the book you have been making or embarking upon. Keep this somewhere you can see it, because we move the goalposts when we achieve something, and it is good to look back. It will help in gentle productivity because it is comforting; you can settle more happily into what windows of time or opportunity you have.

Chapter Twelve

When Hope Is Gone, What Then?

This is a crisis chapter – the next chapter is about difficulty too, but it is more leisurely than this one. But back to this chapter. To write it, I have to tell you about things I did when I was at my lowest – I mean, in terms of creative pursuit. You might feel very low because your entanglements with industry have floored you, or perhaps you are bereaved, very unwell, looking after someone in difficult circumstances or depressed. I cannot offer a specific remedy for those things – and I ought not to, because I am neither a health professional nor a specialist counsellor – so let me share, instead, what I did, and what strategies I used. But bear in mind that sometimes you cannot think positively because something is epically shit. It really hurts. It comes in waves.

Maybe it was a death, a grief, a grief of understanding, like a white light in your mind that you cannot have or be something you always wanted.

The pain from having been deceived, misled or rejected. (WHO would reject YOU? GET ME NAMES IMMEDI-ATELY for my BIG BOOK OF CELTIC GRUDGES.)[23]

---

23 We met these before in the foreword. RAAAAR. (See p. 6.)

Something awful happening to a loved one – your child.

Medical issues, psychological issues, all kinds of intersectional things that go wrong in this truly allistic, ableist world.

Or maybe systems have failed, and continue to fail, around you and you feel you cannot win.

BUT...

In your darkest moments drill down and find a story. I just described things that happened to me recently and which were the stimulus for this book. It's the beginning of a book – or perhaps it's something you are working on. First of all, you have to make the leap of faith and assure yourself creativity works, even when things have gone terribly wrong, even irreparably so; then you begin asking questions about your experience, or something in the room around you (as I did in the chapter on journeys)[24] – or even simpler, think about this: what have I learned that I did not know before, and how could that be a narrative? If what you are going through is terrible, take it away from yourself by keeping the feeling and changing the event, or by imagining the reactions of another person. You have my love as you do this.

Let me share that as I write this chapter I am wishing so hard I could make the pain of one of my children go away, but I cannot; and we have been let down by schools, senior staff members, a university, multiple health professionals and more. There's no point in telling ourselves or others how awful this is – it is plainly awful – so instead I aim to practise emotional thrift, and not make pronouncements on something which is self-evidently ghastly. I hurt – physically, too – around the heart region. I ache as I write this to you, and I am furious. Livid.

---

24 See chapter nine.

I am not going to forgive, either, because half of this is a failure of will – not just people doing the best they can with scant resources, which is also bad, but not so eviscerating, I find.

Drill down.

Ask questions.

Aim for a crystalline thought.

What have I learned? What am I receiving from my senses as I sit with this feeling? How can I turn this harrowing experience into a story? Is there someone here – or some element of the situation – I might satirise, and thus both provide myself with material and render its effect on me just a mote less painful?

An Exercise

Short chapter, short exercise.

Wherever you are now, and however upset, look around you and choose five things – which could include a person if you like. Now, ask a question about one, invent a backstory about another, explore how one impacted on your senses, imagine another upside down and see what you notice and place the final one in a different context – as contrasting as you like. You could write all of these down, giving them a paragraph each.

Something I have always found: telling a story is one way of shaping experience. How would it be if you simultaneously created something beautiful and strengthened yourself by corralling difficult experiences into words? An encouraging thought.

The next chapter takes you further into these themes.

Chapter Thirteen

When the Millstone Becomes the Star[25]

*Unfurling your story in your darkest days. The tiniest
part is still a part of the whole. And grief is
a ball of energy to burn.*

Here is another essay for you. You might want to sit down
for this, because I am going to tell you some stories from my
childhood. In doing so, I want to show you (as in 'Where
There's Shit There's Gold')[26] how you can aim to take that
millstone, all the things in your head and those things lodged
in your body, and write them out. But before I do so, I want
to counsel you again: as you may be touching on a difficult
experience, it can help to put the feelings of these things
and not the actual events into a piece of fiction. You might
change the situation altogether and put the feelings in that
instead, writing in the third person, rather than the first – the
character taking it that step away from you. Or you could use
an alter ego for the same reason.

---

25 I have always loved 'Prelude' by the Northern Irish poet, Patrick
Kavanagh, which this title hints at.
26 See chapter one.

So do you know what you are doing here? You are exploring some things you know in detail, elaborating on them, but you are also taking your millstone and turning it into a star. That does not take the pain away, because loss, grief and suffering are worn and stored, but I have tried to think that, even in my saddest times, I could make something. I believe I had a notion of this at an early age, but could not yet articulate it. I was frightened and angry and trying to get it out, and moulded into different things – and got told off for writing things which were too weird when I was in secondary school.

In the end, I built a setting based on my late father's home in my head; I called it *The Hill*. It was not actually on a hill, but it seemed to be, because it was somehow isolated from everything around it, and in my descriptions, drawing on real and gruesome, baffling events, funnier and funnier things happened at The Hill or were related there at quite staggeringly inappropriate moments: hangings, tumours, enormous rats with giant teeth, an unexploded bomb, repeated lightning strikes, cats with Old Testament names – Simeon, Rastas and Tiresias – locked rooms that no one ever went into – and one of those, I eventually realised, was my grandmother's posh parlour, where she did her seances. I only saw it once, but my imagination grabbed this marvellous room and never let it go, though I was also sad and frightened, because my parents didn't like me very much, so I was always going to be sad and frightened.

My imagination was grabbed by the room – fancy dark-red velvet cushions, tins of things, a plush tablecloth and the smell of damp and death and scary stuff. The whole house took root, in fact, and had much the same ambience.

Let me tell you what else I grabbed: the things from the cupboards and the pantry and the sheds; I hoarded the stories, astounded by their morbidity and their gore. I do not think I was a happy child, or teenager, most of the time, but the point was I knew that, and the fact that I knew that meant I knew what happiness was and, even in this drear place, and within the tensions and, yes, the violence of my family home, that imagination did not fail me. It took up colours and textures and mould-smells and death stories; it took up rustlings that I'd decided came from the seance room: it got so fit and dexterous it worked with other parts of my mind to analyse the weird interplay and the unspoken resentments in the rooms and conversations.

What was there?

There was cruelly boiling tripe with its gusts of steam and laundry-smell; the pantry of frightening pickles, stacked like eyeballs in grandma's dark chamber of horrors. You felt in your bones the damp and the crawling mould. It was a combination of Peggotty's dark storeroom, so frightening to David Copperfield with its smell of 'soap, pickles, pepper, candles and coffee, all at one whiff', and the Salem House schoolroom, with its smell of 'mildewed corduroys, sweet apples wanting air and rotten books.' And, to accompany the odours, there were the stories, recounted over sausages and mash, about the bizarre ways in which Grandpa's brothers had been killed. Off the dark hallway, seeping red cabbage waited for the hard-knuckled hand and downy arm of grandmother to scoop and slop and lay down with less than love, although my imagination told me that she served fondant fancies and not the demon pickles at her seances.

I was convinced that this place had its own weather patterns. Sometimes, in this exposed position on The Hill, which we know wasn't actually on a hill, the wind would whip up, Grandpa's chickens screamed like banshees, timbers creaked and doors quivered and smashed shut: perhaps it was the unquiet souls of the dead, disliking the cheery retellings of their worldly extinction or something to do with the seance room. Grandpa was nearly blind but compensated verbally with story after story; he had never been able to read very much, but he could recite poems by Tennyson and Arnold. But it is said, here's the thing: words can heal; they can make you soar, whether read or heard. And you cannot take them away once they are brought into the world. Sometimes they are good even if a bad person has said them; because they can exist independently of the mouth that uttered them or the horrid geography that spawned them. It is magic.

You know what else is magic? *Your imagination.* Am I saying you cannot write a glorious book because you didn't have a wacko childhood? No. I would be an idiot to say that, and entirely irresponsible. I am trying to show you one source of my stories, and to demonstrate what I did when I was scared.

I stored things in my imagination and rooted around in there later, and so, when people say, 'How on earth did you write nine books in under six years?' then this is how (obviously they didn't all see the light of day). Layer on layer of stories that I had built up.

There is more. Let us fast-forward.

You want to write but you are sad, jaded, lost or ill.

Reach in and see what you can find or look around you and add those two things together, because, even when your life is chaotic, your mind is still there with the capacity to unfurl a tiny story – the tiniest of stories. Start with just a single observation and build it up from there; add a character, a voice, an atmosphere, and linger on them even when you are laid low. Do not push yourself.

I think I need to show you what I mean.

When one of my three sons first became ill, I felt the corners of my world being tugged at, and it is the absolute pits – you will no doubt know this – seeing someone you love suffering. But it was not only that: it was the absolute failure of any professionals that we encountered to help appropriately. I felt a coursing anger and resentment towards those who could have helped and, instead, blamed our family, particularly me, and were accusatory to a young person who was ill. Not malice, of course, but arrogance, allied with a sense that firm decision and firm handling creates a good outcome. Thinking you are doing the right thing may create catastrophe for someone else because, above all, it is the outcome which matters. And listening.

I spent days and nights being watchful and was on high alert for a long time. My health deteriorated. No one would help us, and I felt that happiness had deserted us. But sometimes, when life is awful, you cannot counter awfulness with happiness, because happiness just is not available, so you must counter it with something else. In my case, by gently unrolling a story.

I started looking at paintings of escapes – things that were about freedom. I saw four paintings of a zebra. It was running across London. I immediately started wondering why and how it had escaped and surmised that this was the Blitz. (Correct.) I told more little corners of the story to myself before I looked up the real story, because now I knew there was one. I imagined the origin of this zebra; I pondered a backstory. When I was up at night, exhausted, it came in little snatches, but I kept building. Now I knew the true story: it was a set of paintings by Carel Weight, commissioned by Kenneth Clark, then Director of the National Gallery, in 1947, and the zebra had indeed escaped when its enclosure took a direct hit in the autumn of 1940. In the true event, the animal only got as far as Camden. But as I lay, watchful at night, I imagined where it was born, who and what it knew, what its life was then, what now; I gave it a companion, a child, and then I thought: What if it had not been recaptured but kept running? What then? Where did it go, and who did it meet? Who might steal it – or, rather more interestingly, who might it steal? Those tiny bits of story – just questions and ruminations, really – night after night, in a hazy mind, a tired body, gradually resolved into parts of a storyline. I expect you've already guessed I had the pastel-coloured index cards out as I thought about all the characters in the book!

Gradually, then gently, and yes, sadly, a world was built. The lovely thing was that, as it grew, it became a new world I could go into when I needed to, and this was especially helpful during lockdown, because I had Covid early, followed by Long Covid, and I truly learned what fatigue was for the first time. And my son was not getting better.

I will always be grateful to that zebra and the little pieces of story which emerged, feeling so hopeless, physically, emotionally. And do you know what? When you read this, *The Zebra and Lord Jones* will already be out.

That's how I know that you will slowly, sadly, put together a story… In my case, I brought back all the horrors of my strange childhood experiences – except that they were no longer horrors, but hues and textures and secrets, locked rooms, magical animals: whispers. They were a technicolour adventure in words and, having corralled them all in language, and massaged their form into something different, I was no longer afraid, and had pages of unafraid words.

Hooray.

An Exercise

I am keeping this one deliberately short. It's possible you skipped to this chapter and are feeling rubbish. You will find there is overlap between this chapter and that on dealing with writer's block – that's intentional – and my idea is, as ever, to get you to lay down some good habits for your writing practice that are doable and kind to *you*.

1. Start doodling and cross-hatching, like you're shading. Or draw cubes, then stars. You do not need to be a talented artist – no one is looking. This is just to orient your brain. I like to do this with a fine liner or (don't laugh at me now) a fountain pen with an italic nib, but you use what you have. I rather like brown ink and violet ink. I'm just telling you so you can see what a sad old nerd I am, with an assortment of pens, nibs and ink. You can have a giggle at that. And I might recommend pastel-coloured index cards again here too – or you could use a notebook. The key thing here is thought, pondering.

2. Now move from your doodling and cross-hatching to words that come to you – use words you like; then think about why you like them. You could always do

this with phrases or sayings if you prefer. Just spend some time pondering. For example, if you wrote the word 'pudding', why? It is a lovely sounding word, no? Does it comfort you with its sound or the thought of it? Would it have to be hot or cold? Why? Why is that important to you? Ponder.

3. Now take one of the words or phrases you have pondered and the feelings that are associated with it for you. Now, in your mind, put the feelings and the word somewhere. In a place. See what happens. What crops up in your head? Which encounters? With whom? If you were thinking about pudding, who might be eating that hot (or cold) pudding, and who are they? What are they like? Are they in an unusual place?

4. Think and daydream about the little scenario that is evolving. You might chuck it out altogether or try another and then, if you feel up to it, try writing a paragraph in a little sprint for ten minutes involving these things. See what happens. You are starting to unfurl stories: have faith that they can come from the least promising place, from a bad mood, a word.

5. As with anything in the book, I would love to know what came of this – so we have created a forum for *The Alchemy*, to which you can add thoughts, responses, progress and news. Stay tuned.

Apologies: this was longer than I thought, but that's because *you're immense* – even when you feel small.

Chapter Fourteen

When You Want to Give Up

Do, then do not.

I asked writers and would-be writers about giving up and there was a thread of argument which I particularly liked – that when self-doubt emerges, you could consider engaging with the struggle because it could well be that the uncertainty is a source of strength, of resource in disguise. Eighteen months ago, I almost gave up writing. I had wanted to write for decades; that I did not is connected to how I nearly gave up, and why I want to ensure you keep at it. However, I think it's important to say sometimes it is really OK to give up for a while, to throw in the towel, if you are feeling so stressed, intimidated or worried about your own ability – whether those feelings seem, to you, to be coming from within or because of harsh things that were said to you. Also, it is also fine, isn't it, to give up if you really need to?

My lovely late friend Richard once said to me that it helps to ask yourself if you are running away from something or running to it. I have never forgotten that maxim. You can run towards a place of greater safety and peace, as it seems to you. Even then, there are ways of gently keeping the doors open in terms of creative practice – and we will come to that in a moment, in the exercise at the end of the chapter.

I see frankly heroic people querying agents for years and not getting a request for a full manuscript. I also see writers in fury and sad because their work is not valued as it might be, or because they get their hopes up and find themselves ghosted by the publisher or agent who requested their full manuscript or indie publisher who had shown passionate interest. I know this happens, because people write me emotional messages about it, or ring me in tears, and I have done so with others. Publishing is a tough industry. I feel weird saying that, because my grandfathers were down the mines and lost digits, and to say that writing and publishing are tough seems a bit embarrassing – a bit performative. Nonetheless, you are making things and trying to put them out there, and it makes you feel vulnerable. Of course it does. We might as well own that one now.

I felt discouraged, being told I was lucky to get published at all, called arrogant and guilty of talking about myself too much. I also had a couple of experiences where people in the industry, who seemed to be lauded for their community spirit, inclusion and professionalism elsewhere, told me that I was rubbing the noses of other people with mental-health problems in it all. This was the most destabilising thing for me, because I had sought to be open about my experience in order that the next person – even if it was only one person – felt less embarrassed or less alone. We should not feel this way, but we do. If any sense of shame I had been carrying had lessened, it came back in spades now. These things were going on during the pandemic, while we were all so stretched, fearful and uncertain and, in our case, while one of our older children was also seriously ill – given the circumstances, help and support were harder to find than usual. I will not complain, because it was hard for everyone, but naturally ingesting criticism of this nature further destabilised me. I had two books out that first pandemic year, and had felt so excited, but now I doubted my ability, thought I was disliked within the industry and was not sure where I was going next. I kept it moving on social media, though, looking gainfully employed – but all the time I was worrying, Do I look cocky? Am I talented?

If you spend a few minutes on socials and hanging out in writers' groups, you will meet many people who think they ought to give up, but don't truly want to, who think they might have played it wrong, who are tired.

But you need to know what I did next.

I put a call out on Twitter.[27] I said that I would appreciate a chat with experienced authors – and boy, did they come. I am aware that some not very edifying behaviour occurs in our industry, but there is so much good too, and it does not advertise itself. I had email conversations, got checked on during the week, had long phone calls. I was worried that I looked needy, but I am so glad that I was open: about writing and how my history and personal circumstances made me feel vulnerable. About why it took me so long to write in the first place.

So that is my first tip. Ask for help if you want to give up. Contextualise it – and ask me if you do not know who else to ask. Be bold.

---

27 Yes, yes, it's X now, but we call it Twitter anyway, don't we?

Now, I began to think about the barriers that had stopped me writing in the first place, to consider first how this made industry experience triggering, then how I might use this experience – sustained trauma, mental-health problems over decades and latterly chronic physical issues and being a carer, and the challenging awakening all this was having – and take it forward in a book to empower others. Yes, of course I needed to take the time to reflect on things I was getting wrong, and to check my communication, and I discussed this. Then I approached several writers I admired, and I asked them if they would collaborate with me. I spoke to my agent about how I was feeling and what I could do. You may not be agented, in which case aim to find a person who knows you and your work – and do not be ashamed. I was encouraged to find a resolution: to turn my anger and upset into a ball of energy; to direct it towards writing and joy. This, incidentally, is how the *Bookseller* column I wrote for a year came about – and then that for *Mslexia*. How all the short pieces – a varied bunch – came about because, buoyed up, I pitched various pieces, had two taken up, and my style and content hit a note and I began to branch out more. The thrust of this, from the beginning, was robust help and empowerment, insofar as I could offer it from a modest platform.

That done, I put another call out on Twitter, asking if an industry professional could have a chat with me. Something amazing happened: I made a new friend – someone, a writer and editor, who had stacks of insight and who helped me plan for wider industry work, suggesting who to approach, considering my teaching background. I got some wonderful classes and teaching, and just as I did that, I got a call from an academic (of whom I was in awe) asking me to make a podcast with her. Other opportunities followed. Finally, I started work again on a novel, insisting to myself I could do it: *The Zebra and Lord Jones*. I wrote a memoir, plus a proposal, a book of essays, a novella that I am developing and spoke about a non-fiction proposal, a cultural history, not daring to believe there would be interest: news of that to be revealed. Meanwhile, another non-fiction book that had gone out from my agency did not sell, so I evolved the plan and applied for Arts Council England funding. I did not get the funding, so I took the spirit of the book, which would have been an anthology of various writers, and began again, making a book that was for you, from me.

You are reading it now. It is called *The Alchemy* for more than one reason. Way leads on to way. A book of essays is going to be published in 2024, I started a new literary prize for writer-carers and industry supported it brilliantly, so we have its anthology out. AND FINALLY, quite possibly by the time you are reading this, I will be back at university, doing a year-long PhD by Published Works, using my own books, on magical realism and trauma.[28]

Do you see how, step by step, this is all connected?

So, remember: if rejection or others' diminishment of you have made you want to give up, pause and reflect. Is there something you are doing and need to examine? That done,

---

28 For context: *These Envoys of Beauty: A Memoir* (Abingdon: Reflex Press, 2023); *The Zebra and Lord Jones* (London: Renard Press, 2023); *The Curae* (London: Renard Press, 2023); *To Melt the Stars: Essays about Love* (Talgarreg: Broken Sleep Books, 2024). My PhD thesis is: 'Go there on a wing in your imagination: Magical Realism as therapeutic writing in *Saving Lucia* and *These Envoys of Beauty* (York St John University).

take your sadness and go forth. Help others along the way. Find people who bolster you and your work and give it back in spades. Doubt is a good thing: it is a function of both intellect and morality. But if that doubt is eviscerating, it has gone too far. Start building and calling on your tribe. Don't have one? You can always start with me. You can build from there. I want to tell you too that these plans and thoughts were evolved by little conversations and teary chats, in a bubble bath and on a walk or resting – twice in an MRI scanner, and on one of those occasions after I had pressed the panic button because I was scared about my body and wearing a head clamp over a mask. *Think of something else*, said the technician, putting on a CD. It was Ed Sheeran. The time before that Gary Barlow. I said, *Please will you turn off the Sheeran*, put the headphones back on, closed my eyes and *clank, clank, clank,* I thought good thoughts about this book; I thought about how I would want to be spoken to and the things I had wanted someone to tell me and be with me for; I have tried to place these at the heart of this book. They crystallised in the MRI scanner, and I came out and cried on my husband because I was pleased I had had that thought – but I knew my typing was all over the place and my balance was defective.

You don't need the perfect space. You don't need the perfect body – who has that anyway? What is it? I will be lopsided and a bit dribbly, and that's just how it is. If you see me dribbling at an event, or a bit teary, or needing to sit down, just hand me a tissue and possibly a cup of tea and we will just continue.

I didn't give up – but I did give up some things, some people and some directions. I began thinking that what I needed, above all, was creative endeavour, and this surrounded the books as part of a portfolio career, or what I came to regard as One Big Creative Project.[29] Accruing online teaching; articles; online mentoring. They exist because of the books, and build up around them, step by step.[30] But you know, the letting go of things, the realising you cannot have what you hoped, need to be grieved for, so cut loose, get off social media and allow yourself to grieve a bit. I did that too, and for a while my eldest son and my husband tweeted for me. Team effort: I had to rest by being quieter for a while.

An Exercise

Say you have been chipping away at a book or querying it with a litter of rejections or (I find this worse) no replies or (is this the worst?) requests for full manuscripts then radio silence. If this is depleting you or making you feel you need a break from your book, I want to suggest this: isolate the key theme or themes from your book — you could get out

---

29 Particular credit goes to author and commissioning editor Abbie Headon for prompting me here. At a low point, she gave me gentle, good-humoured nudges and helped me make a new template: this was hugely liberating, and I will always be grateful. All creatives need people like Abbie in their lives, I think!

30 A book that has helped me is *The Kaizen Way* by Robert Maurer (see chapter five) — it talks about the concept of great change being made through small steps: ask small questions, think small thoughts, take small actions, solve small problems — the idea being that small steps circumvent the brain's resistance to new behaviours. In other words, trick your cortex. I find this approach positive — relaxing, even — and it was particularly comforting when one of my sons was so ill and I had little rest for eighteen months. It's all about essential little increments of productivity, and you are still moving forward.

those pastel-coloured index cards I mentioned, then write the theme/themes on the cards and let your mind wander.

How might that theme/each of those themes form a short story? Jot down a few thoughts on each card. You might prefer to think, instead, towards a non-fiction piece. Do the same on a new card. Other things you could consider with the work in hand: how might you construct a short story around one of the characters in your book – perhaps where things work out differently? If you have been putting together a collection of short stories, is it possible that events or the life of a character in one of your short stories could be extended into a novella or novel? Or is there a particular section of a story that could be expanded into one? Put one or all of these thoughts down on the cards – just things to make you think. And of course, you need not write – you could record voice notes, for example. The point is that I am encouraging you, yet again, to use what you have, and to do it in a gently productive way. You might call it literary recycling. Personally, I have had to employ this technique to maximise on the work I have already done, because of caring responsibilities, fatigue and inconsistent health.

Oh, but there's another reason why I am asking you to do this other than for thrift and energy conservation.

When you want to give up, but you enjoy the writing, keep your hand in by experimenting with other media. If you have written a novel, try a short story or a non-fiction piece – that's what I was getting you to think about in this chapter when you wrote on the index cards. I stalled after writing two novels and a novella, and that is when I wrote my first short-story collection and (using what you have, remember?) I incorporated elements of memoir and took real events and transposed them in some way, and it helped me to have them in a themed collection. The book came together quite easily that way, and I wrote a story a day, so there was a draft collection in under a month. I worked in little bursts of ten minutes, twenty minutes, half an hour, because that was what I had at that point. That may not seem like gentle productivity to you, but the truth was that I already had a lot of the material in my head, so the next step was to make it into short (and very short) stories. If you have tried this exercise, let me know how you got on. Find me on socials or add it to the forum: I see *The Alchemy* as a book, but also as a method: a community.

Chapter Fifteen

Hitting a Hard Place

How are you? I am mostly OK, and that is because I am doing well in thinking of the day only in increments, pausing and limiting stress as best as I can, sitting with and observing tricky things, and seeing them, mostly, pass.

I am an English teacher, a young people's mentor, writer and mother. Mental-health problems are part of my history and of who I am. I am very open about this, in the hope that it will make it easier for the next person to be so too. But I am autonomous, and these things do not define me – they may do so in others' eyes sometimes, but not in mine. Don't let them define YOU too if you also manage these pesky things – it makes them easier to tolerate, and thus you can begin to ignore others' opinions. And don't ever let anyone persuade you that you cannot write because you have difficulty in corralling your thoughts or emotional life. The industry has its demands, that's for sure – so go easy on yourself and curate some sturdy self-belief if you possibly can. When rejected, be cross, but don't brew that awful feeling of persecution that will stymie all creativity – speaking from experience there!

I have written elsewhere about mental-health problems. I have a history of them: generalised anxiety, major depression and then OCD in late childhood and adolescence. I have dissociative episodes, which are scary and unpleasant and, from time to time, I wake at night with vivid dreams and flashbacks.

This last weekend was dislocated by a number of difficult episodes and Sunday was spent in a jumble of senses and feelings; things become much more acute: words burn – but then, so does beauty. I have had some wonderful care, although am not sure I will ever be entirely better – but that's OK. I make this point in my 2020 novel, *Saving Lucia*: that you can still go out into the world and be creative and do things when fragile, faltering, imperfect and not entirely well. Human beings are messy and absolute brilliant at failure, anyway! I must add, in case someone who is really struggling is reading this and thinking that they cannot do this and what a failure they are, that I have had all areas of my working and creative life curtailed by mental-health problems, but we carry on – and help each other to. I imagine that if I had been supported and appropriate help was found for me in earlier years, things would have been different, and could be different now. That's a bit sad, so I turn it outwards and imagine that perhaps my not being fixable has helped me to be a better teacher or writer – or perhaps better able to help others – especially young people – in need and distress, or just a tangle. What is more, I have distilled from problems and from mental-health crises some colourful material, a character or two and even a book (my first one).

Now, my situation has gradually got more complex, owing to additional needs and unmet needs within my immediate family, so I have additional caring and teaching needs at a busy time. I am just raising my head from a fog of exhaustion because some of those needs were met during the night for months, and even when I was not needed – well, I have been in a state of hyper-vigilance for the best part of a year with little respite. In addition to this, I have experienced what could euphemistically be described as unhelpful behaviour around me – from health and education providers and related agencies – and it has cut to the heart of who I am. Some of it was also triggering because it reminded me on a visceral level of my mother's worst excesses. My reaction was physical; I was doubled over – my body unable to process what I was hearing and seeing and finding myself swatted back to an earlier pathology and, with my worries about my family, who were rather caught up in it all, experiencing grief. Oh, but even in grief, on your darkest day, you can start asking questions and so unfurl a story. This is what I found. I would allow myself to feel the feeling and aim to note it and pause – not denying it, but attempting to breathe into it – and then I would start imagining a poem, or a short story, or the beginning of a novel, asking questions about feelings, situations, people; the things I could see in hospital waiting rooms.

How about you? What if you are managing others' needs and your own are rattling round and you want to make something – or to feel better? This is what I do. This is specifically about writing, but maybe some thoughts here are helpful for anything!

This year – 2023 – alone, I will have three books, one translation (in which I was wonderfully involved) and the anthology resulting from the literary prize I inaugurated out.

In addition to this, I had various other short pieces and a major column published. Not every year can be like this, and I do not suggest it is a target or there is anything special about me but listen: comments were made last week by a handful of people on social media who said I should not mention this level of activity, because it is unrealistic for most people. I have also previously been told that it is wrong – readers will not know who or *what* I am if I am prolific or varied – or that I cannot be being careful or editing properly with an output like this. Well, this is my reality, and the thing is, for most of my adult life, I have not had the confidence to do it. I've seen things go down the drain and – I want to say this because I have previously been ashamed – I have twice, because of mental illness, not finished a PhD. TWICE. So, any comment I make about what I am doing is in the context of a skip-load of failure (a word which I would qualify, anyway).

So this level of activity occurs at least in part because it was stopped up for so long.

Ah – I might have lost you: share your success, whatever it is, and to be proud of it, because you've done it in extremis. I don't mean brag, I mean share. Also, your method, or degree of volition or propulsion, will be unique to you, so please be encouraged to be true to yourself.

Also, may I? To industry folk who think it is acceptable to say there is only one way to be, to publish, to write, fuck off to a bookshop and then fuck out the other side and keep fucking off (please remember to pause to buy a book or two).

That nagging voice in your head that says you can't write because… YES: there are things in the writing business that quite clearly need to change. *Obviously* there are. But for everything else, is the voice in your head yours? Are you putting yourself down all the time? I do it too but have learned to listen and say 'Stop!' Challenge that voice, because it's trying it on, frankly. For me, I think the voice that chimes in is mostly my Ma telling me what a worthless little creature I am. Listen, then escort out. Now try telling yourself something different with that voice. When I do that, my shoulders go back, and I feel a lift in my energy levels.

Write.

Just do it and at whatever speed.

It will be awful, but that is because it's your Frankendraft: your shit first draft. Your crappy first paragraphs.

Still, this is how a short story or novel gets started. You are going to cross most of it out, but no part of this process is wasted. If you are having a tough day, try to do this. If not, read a bit, think a bit, research a bit. It's all work.

If you are a carer in some capacity, really try to box up a bit of attention just for yourself. If your child is in a hole, do NOT get in the hole with them, because you will make yourself ill. I know this because I have. Creativity is one release for you here, and I have found, counter-intuitively, that the fact I don't have much time forces the words out. Don't wait for ideal conditions. They may never come.

Step it up. Try to move, if you can. If you can't afford gym membership or a class, do it at home, and do at least some of it outside if you possibly can. For me, the breathing and discipline of Pilates is great, and it makes me stronger and better able to deal with difficulty. There are loads of free resources online. I am acutely aware as I write that exercise is not possible for all, so please be forgiving of me and do what is right and possible for you – and then you could share with others what that was.

Lean on the (writing) tribe I mentioned earlier – and let me remind you that this tribe might be online. Twitter is a great resource for writers (not the only one, but it's my preferred route and I'd advise exploring BookTok[31] and seeing how it all feels), though I don't think any evidence suggests that a lot of Twitter activity will shift books – unless you do non-fiction and your posts are all about that, for a platform. So don't feel under pressure: engage on your own terms, mute and curate as you need to. Make something for your own support.

Don't feel bad if you don't write every day. You are still a proper writer – enough of this tyranny already! Also, think – always and without exception – in terms of observing detail. It's soothing and stimulating. I take pictures too. Leaves, an interesting hat, the shift of a tree in the breeze to an unusual angle, buildings, stone, walls, streetscapes, faces, overheard conversations. Be observant, and I do believe that, as well as feeling better, you will find that stories rise up to meet you. Be ready for them.

Do not assume that those who don't have your problems don't have any problems. Some people's lives are easier. But yours is the only one you have – and look at you: you're a stone-cold miracle there. Don't assume that other people have it sussed. And when you see writing types who seem

---

31 You probably know this, but this is the book bit of TikTok, and it is frequently rather wonderful and we have come to learn that TikTok has become a major driver of sales. As with all things – Bookstagram on Instagram, say – if you try it out, make things and that feels OK, go forth. If it makes you feel nervous, edgy or uncomfortable, take a break or do not start. Your mental health, your well-being and the physical health which is so tightly bound up with it are more precious. If you need permission not to indulge on those grounds, I just handed it to you.

particularly confident and want some of that, it is likely that they are blagging it or... just maybe... they are a bit cocky – in which case, I will wager that this is not the best for writing or the careful lifting-up of others.

Read. Lose yourself in a book. Read *different* books. I have built and rebuilt my mind with reading, and I fervently hope that it can be this way for you too, if you need it.

I wish you love and courage,

Anna

Exercises

This is very short, but I want the notion of the naysaying voices in your head – and telling them off – to be the cornerstone, OK? Also, I worry I might already have spent this chapter telling you what to do, barking exercises! But this is important and draws on what we covered before when I was talking to you about love and self-talk.

Whose voice is in your head? Is it your shit ex-husband or wife, some gaslighter acquaintance, someone who is bitter and takes it out on you, an overly critical parent? That's their voice telling you you're no good and WHO DO YOU THINK YOU ARE writing this book? It's not your voice; it's *theirs*. I bet you would not allow this to be said, this level of discouragement, to someone else, so don't echo it back to yourself. Remember to be kind in what you say to yourself, praise yourself gently for creative endeavour and support your own efforts. That is your exercise. Challenge the nagging thought with a good thing about your book. You can start with the fact that you are making something exist which did not before, and that is an amazing thing.

This done, I want you to go out into the world – or on social media, blog, newsletter, or wherever your pleasure is – and pay it forward. Notice, support, encourage and compliment other writers – creatives, more broadly speaking, too. They seem fine to you? These are curated environments, and you can only see a tiny slice of what is lived. There will be many people who are not encouraged and positively rewarded, and how would you know?

A while ago, I complimented someone in a shop on her pink hair. It was what we now call Millennial Pink, so a dusty, rosy, pale shade of pink, sitting somewhere between Barbie pink and rose quartz. Anyway, I told her I thought it was gorgeous, because it was. Then I felt embarrassed. She did not react at all, and I felt I had been forward, possibly a bit weird. Not a bit of it: she was just composing her thoughts; and she said, 'That is the first compliment I have had.'

'What, on your hair?' I said. 'Oh, people are just unobservant, or can be shy.'

'No, that is the first compliment I think I have *ever* received. I mean, about *anything*.'

Now, maybe it was, or maybe it was the first which went in. It did not matter. We were both smiling.

Perhaps she even wrote a story one day.

Chapter Sixteen

Thoughts about Industry, Morale

and Self-Worth

Now, I want to try and make those feeling sad or disenfranchised a little better. I base my observations on my own experience over the past six years, and that which has been generously shared with me by others. How is this part of gentle productivity – or even the most furious productivity? Well, I would argue that a degree of sustained upset chips away, and that being demeaned, however subtly, over a period can be eviscerating, especially if you keep it to yourself. So to work with what you have, as I described it at the beginning of the book, you don't need a goblin – or his mates – at your elbow. You don't need a goblin who tells you they know best what's right for you because they are an industry expert, yet at the same time they make you uncomfortable. Trust your instinct here. Use my guidelines below to know if you're being had, and please remember that there is, as is any industry, some bad behaviour, and some goblin behaviour – but it is not the majority of those in the industry. It can be difficult to believe when those goblins are also nice to kittens or mobilise for good social things – but remember that the Krays were really hot on charity work, but also boiled people in oil – and there I have failed to sustain the extended goblin metaphor.

Let us start with bullying. To define this: if someone has become nervous or frightened of an individual or individuals – more broadly of the industry and the world around them, because make no mistake this bleeds into our broader lives – because of repeated unsettling or undermining behaviour towards them, this is bullying.

Have I been bullied? Indeed. I almost stopped writing because of it.

I was worried about speaking to people, but I had no choice. I am vulnerable, and I get ill; I come from a complex trauma background. If I had not ultimately found support, you would not be reading this. I still got things done, but for over two years it was jerky and unsatisfactory; I stopped enjoying my writing, and my self-worth was much reduced; gentle productivity felt inadequate: I felt if I did not push, push, push, it would end. This did not work.

So I am still here. Fractured but furious. I know this, and much worse, has happened to others. I know, from shared stories, that others have encountered gaslighting, silencing, or had their work passed off as another's. None of this is acceptable. Would it were possible to see more structure in place so that industry professionals were governed by a code of conduct, with a conduit to reasonable and over-arching support and redress. Sometimes industry professionals tweet about the things that *everyone knows* when stories erupt following a sustained pattern of unpleasant behaviour. Truly, only a small pool of people *do* know, and those beyond the pool may feel disquieted – even frightened. Firm discussion and careful handling of social media, particularly Twitter threads, are helpful here, although

I truly understand how these patterns occur. Thinking more about Twitter, surely it behoves no one in our industry to pit sectors against one another, because all it does is make things look more unsafe – particularly to people who struggle to find a voice. I am mindful, for example, of publishers being openly critical of others' practice. Moreover, hashtags used by organisations – '#kindness' is one which particularly makes me want to be sick on my feet – need to be treated with caution by the recipient. Why? Because core values are not performative, and declarations of rectitude in this context *may* be a deflection when poor practice is taking place behind the scenes. I worry: there are vulnerable people out there.

It's time to tell you what I did when I was on the floor so that we can make sure it does not happen to you.

First, I established a mutually supportive writing tribe – online – around myself; then I asked for help online openly and was stunned to have people emailing me and asking to call me at home – and I am speaking partly of some well-known writers. Heartening, isn't it? Then I spoke to an organisation: if you are being treated badly – even if you are unsure what constitutes bad behaviour and need to talk over your situation – find a professional who can advise. Here are three unions:

The Society of Authors (SoA):
www2.societyofauthors.org

The Writers' Guild of Great Britain (WGGB):
writersguild.org.uk

The National Association of Writers in Education (NAWE):
www.nawe.co.uk

Then, with a quality of grudge that thrives in the Celt, I fought back and – take a deep breath now – relaxed and went back to the idea of being gently productive. Prolific, as we have established.

So here are some things to think about to build a healthy world around you, as best you can. This might be when you are thinking about publication, signing a contract or even looking to extricate yourself. First, when there's no dialogue offered, or you try to open up dialogue and find it's impossible: beware. Someone I know had a publication date change three times without their being informed. Someone else has had barely any contact with their publisher, surely a *baseline* requirement. Another asked some questions and was told that they were dealing with an expert who knew exactly what they were doing and that was that. If it runs like a covert operation, then pause. *Raise your sights*. You are not the last turkey in the shop. Moreover, if your health declines, or that of the people around you; or if you are nervous or stuck in your work, you ought to be able to tell your publisher, editor or agent. This is being open and professional – not weak.

If you cannot get answers to key questions, that's of concern. It is reasonable to talk about publicity, editing or where your book might be sold. This is art, but it is also commerce, so know, for example, whether your travel costs are covered for a book event, and how you will ALL work to maximise sales. Another important point is that you do some looking about. Is there little parity between the publisher's or agent's authors (clients) when you look at social media and elsewhere? Probe to find out if some authors are invisible. Caveat: bear in mind that no two people have the same experience with a press, publisher, agent or editor, so if it feels to you as if it will work, then be wary of making too many comparisons, because you are unique. There are areas of subjectivity, and there are always variables.

If you are working, or hoping to work, with a publisher – I might say particularly an independent press run by one or two people, where it could be difficult for you, as an author, to manage if someone is both founder and publisher and has a deep emotional attachment to what they have created, which might not, ultimately, be to the advantage of the author – please take heart at all times, and make sure you value yourself. Check that at least some of their back catalogue is available. If it is not, try to find out why. At some point *you* will be back catalogue. Your work has value; moreover, it ought to have some longevity in its availability and visibility. Again, you ought to be able to ask about this without anyone making you feel demanding or like a prima donna. Then – and this might be contentious – keep an eye out for vocabulary used, and how it might obscure problems. What do I mean here? That referring to a business relationship in terms of your being part of a 'cohort' or 'family' can be problematic, because, while you're united by your love of books, it suggests a blurring of lines somewhere, and that might not be to your advantage in terms of commerce; also, it might be a highway to exploitative behaviour.

Of course, I might also feel this is uncomfortable because my feelings about family and its structures are complex. I love to work with people, and I love art and the feeling of shared endeavour that goes with it: it can make me feel so alive. I want it to be friendship, but there must also be clearly defined and therefore respectful – and, importantly, profitable – business terms: I would argue that in some cases the family notion smudges those tenets. Having said this, due diligence can show you where it is a genuine thing: mutual support, to help us all be in the same boat, rowing upstream. There are some excellent examples of this degree of unity across the industry – and all the more reason to rout out disingenuous practice.

Something I find deeply concerning, now that I know a bit more about the industry and about my limits, is if the person or publisher you've been offered a contract with is frequently and openly critical of other parts of the publishing industry: beware. I DO NOT mean those champions aiming to improve diversity; I mean those who verbally attack agents, big publishers, other publishers, genres of literature. Who say that publishing is a dangerous place, without supporting contextual data. Remember, they who cries danger is sometimes the danger in plain sight. It can be a function of gaslighting: not assuring you of safe harbour in a storm, but saying they are the only safe harbour in that storm. Likewise, if someone tells you they are your only chance of being published, RUN – or at least SASHAY slowly away (this being a book on gentle productivity). This is power-mongering, gaslighting. Publishing is, it seems to me, a series of gains and losses. Of life-changers and bad track; of having to deal with carping, walking egos – but also finding yourself lifted up by kind and brilliant people. This could mean fewer options for you as avenues are closed off, but...

With an agent or a publisher, make sure you are given a good contract, and that it is explained to you. If it isn't – or if any concerns are waved away – that should be a big red flag. Join a union – see above. Get your contract vetted by them, a perk of membership of the Society of Authors and the Writers' Guild.[32] Also, if you have given someone a contracted second book and two years later you have no answer, reconsider. That is unreasonable. Publishing moves slowly, but there's slow and... *they're really not that into you* slow. While we are talking about the Society of Authors and others, do note that they will be able to advise you if codes or legal clauses have been breached. Opacity is a red flag – and not knowing what is going on and feeling you have no redress make you feel powerless. And finally, *if you feel uncomfortable*, that is a huge red flag. If someone or something makes you feel uncomfortable, I urge you to trust your gut. If you feel intimidated, put down, mocked or – God forbid – frightened, get out. Yes, *even if it seems OK for everyone else*. Bullies are nice to some people, authors do not necessarily speak up if they have been in a similar situation and sometimes people will act out of self-interest. Please look after yourself and get some support. Again, I have found my union very understanding, comforting and proactive in this area.

Just to reiterate, although this is a book about writing, I want to think in terms of context and the ways in which you need to look after yourself so the rest can work. I hope this has all made sense. In terms of what you might add, the single most helpful thing for me has been the communities I have bound myself to. I do not actually have an in-person writing group, but have met other writers on social media, and been particularly drawn to those who have a campaigning spirit and those who are working alongside chronic health problems and other challenges which, while consistently there, present many variables and inconsistencies to deal with. So we chat

---

32 See chapter sixteen.

regularly, support one another and I also have a little tribe of people who are my 'writing support group' and all there – health, wealth and writing – is shared in kind confidence.

You may say, 'I am so shy: I couldn't gather groups of people around me like that!' You know what I say to that? I am awkward, a bit shy, socially gauche, and not particularly sophisticated (I also fall over my own feet), and I truly believe that if I can do it, you can. And as I say, I am well aware that not everyone has the wherewithal, funds or health to go out and about and meet book people, so if you need to keep it online and in very short bursts because your life has to be predicated on rest, then do just that. Set your own parameters because your life is not less worthy or rich than anyone else's. I think, though, that it is strengthening to build a small community around yourself, remembering that as you do this, you are also enabling others to thrive.

An Exercise

Find some writers you really like through reading their work and watching how they engage in social media. This is not the only way to connect, but it was the only way I had open to me, so I share it with you. Engage with them on social media – and I think Twitter would be your best bet here. You might, for example, note writers who seem to have a sensibility like yours. Then, ask them if they would like to be in a writing group with you. A writing group need not only be where you share and critique one another's work; it may also be a support group for those within the industry and/or trying to access the industry. For me, the regular sharing and commenting on work would be too much, which is why I – we – have what we have. You can offer links to anything you publish of course, but for me – us – it is much more about connection, empathy, asking for and sharing advice and showing one another what we are reading. My group is called 'Writing Support Group' for that reason. So, give it a little while, then DM a few people and see if they'd like to be in a little cohort with you. Try it. You might be surprised how readily others will connect, and they may be so pleased you asked: you never know how little or how much support another has, because what you see on social media or in the media is curated, so it may make their day that you asked. People often feel invisible; powerless – but you can do something about that. Yeah, you.

Chapter Seventeen

Thoughts from Others

This chapter is special, and I know for a fact that some of the thoughts I am about to share are from writers and would-be writers seeing their words in print for the first time – and I am listening and asking you, reader, to attend.

Let me explain.

In the UK alone, there are thought to be about seven million carers; to paraphrase the definition given by the National Health Service, a carer is anyone, including children[33] and adults, who looks after a family member, partner or friend who needs help because of their illness, frailty, disability, a mental-health problem or an addiction and cannot cope without their support. The care they give is unpaid. Because of this scale, and because of my own history, in 2022 I established a prize, the Curae, for writer-carers, to help give them voice, then give them a

---

33 There are thought to be around 800,000 young carers in the UK – that is, those under the age of eighteen. I used to be one but, like many people in this role, did not understand that I was; but this is a whole other story.

platform to amplify their voice, but also to provide steps into the industry if that was what was wanted. And access. Outreach. That is partly what *The Alchemy* is about, of course. So I asked all entrants the following question, and asked their permission to include a selection of their comments in this book:[34]

> *'Tell me, in a few sentences, HOW you write a little in tough circumstances; maybe even on the worst days?'*

Their responses were incredible, and I'd like to share them with you. You can see strategy here, and proof that solace is drawn from creativity. Importantly, the writing is not only done in small increments, but sometimes in longer sessions, sometimes spontaneously when demands lapse for a while; and it may be grabbed with both hands if that's what feels right. Be ready for those sessions, too, if you like – or hope for a combination of both, keeping in mind what I outlined at the beginning of this book: always work with what you have. Something else to bear in mind is comfort: these are small things that make a significant difference to how you feel as you set to work. Be gentle on yourself and don't neglect these things – whether it is a favourite blanket or a hot drink in a mug with a particularly jaunty bee on it. What is it for you? These things, because they are investments in your well-being, are also investments in your writing – and, if you really need it, here is permission from me.

---

34 I would have liked to include them all, but the number of entrants far exceeded my expectations.

I have offered comments on what the Curae entrants have shared where it seemed helpful to expand on a point or show you how you – or I – might apply an idea in practical terms. Remember: *be comforted*. Everyone you are about to hear from is writing in challenging conditions. They are not all working on a book, but they are all writing *in extremis*. What became clear as entries for the Curae came in was that many entrants were also chronically ill or had a disability, which made their caring work trickier. Have a look. I have found the following comments supportive, and I hope that you will, too.

> Maybe without life changing as it did and taking me down this winding path which seems to have no end or direction, I wouldn't be writing. For all it had taken away it's also given me this different life – slower, gentler, more reflective. Sadder too, of course, but those flashes of joy are all the more precious for their brevity.
>
> Kate Durrant

How about *that* for a unique way of looking at things? Nobody is saying 'better this way' here – that would be trite, ableist and damaging. However, I would also echo a phrase from earlier: try to see, however tentatively, that with limits come new possibilities. I know that this is what I have done.

Despite the utter exhaustions of the day, sleep eludes me. I switch on my lamp and write in my notebook. In the morning I read the ideas born out of the darkest hours, and this helps me face a new day.

Christine Holt

I think there is something bolstering in this. You salvage just a little something from tender moments and, in doing that, strengthen yourself to do it again – and maybe do more, too.

When I find odd moments to write, in an endless schedule of to-dos, which must be done by me and me alone, I am at my happiest. My mind is then no longer filled with incessant noise.

R. Tesfaiohannes

This resonates with me, and I hope it shall with you, too. There is, in writing, and in progressing with a long piece of work, an act of trust. That you will continue to step forward. Not only that, but the absorption is respite and, if your nerves jangle and you race ahead – what if, what next, how will I – and on and on – you can relax into some work. I would tentatively suggest that my focus now, with greater demands on me, is actually better; I am less distracted and, because I am working away in my head a great deal, some of the work is already done, and it's a relief and sense of accomplishment to set it down.

For me, writing a little does not work, because once I'm in my stride, I have to keep the momentum going, sometimes for several hours. This means I write when my child is at a day centre, because he needs my constant attention when he is at home. No social media, no housework, no distractions of any kind, and I can achieve a great deal, which encourages me to carry on when the next window of opportunity presents itself.

Dee Gordon

Straight from the lion's mouth, then: sometimes productivity is snatched and played out over several hours, because that's where the gap is. Also, note what Dee has shared about the window of opportunity which presents itself. She is alive to that possibility and is happy to grab it, and doing so supports her doing it again.

I find my days are taken up with clutter and noise from my duties around the home, and others coming and going; I find my time to write is in the early hours, when the environment is quiet: I will either read or write up until about 3 a.m., before I sleep. It is only in those few hours I can gather my thoughts and write notes and concepts. To type, I endeavour to do so when I can during slack periods of the day when they appear.

Derek Penn

You can see here how working with what you have is key. Is it perfect, or easy? It's far from it, but the way in which this time has been curated is, dare I say it, inspirational. It's also about spotting time when it appears and seeing what you might do in that time.

My inspiration comes from a germ of an idea, which, like a vegetable, slowly grows. I mull it around in my head, often for weeks, and then comes the moment to write. If stuck, sit down at your keyboard and simply write something – for example, What did you do yesterday? What might you be looking forward to? Write anything and then focus on what you really want to write. It works.

Alan Grant

I find this one so comforting. Do you? Just ease yourself into work with the most mundane thing, if necessary, then take it forward, if you can – maybe by making a more complex question or trying the same question in different ways.

On my difficult days, I make myself a hot chocolate and start to mind-map the idea that has come into my head. Using brightly coloured felt-tip pens makes my paper stand out, and I then carry on writing at least three lines while in my thick pyjamas and with my blanket over me.

Jodie Bishop

Attend to your comfort and the things that make your body feel better. I always write notes and do edits in coloured felt-tip. Also, try mind-mapping. You can do this is many ways.[35]

The next one is longer. I was offered two and kept them both:

I am lopsided from carrying needs. Often, I fall. Limbs folding inwards, I collapse and curve and curl into a corner of the floor. Any corner. Any floor. I fade. I cry. I am no one.

---

35 Tony Buzan is the king of mind-mapping. You might try any of his books.

And yet. A word lolls in my mind and my mouth. Raw, rough, and uncertain. It softens and smoothes. Takes on a shape and a meaning and a life. Another. More. I scribble them on to paper. Tap notes into a phone. Type half a page in Word. And I unfurl. I stand. I am light and I am free. I am someone.

The most difficult times are when exhaustion has drained any hope I might have in my writing or my creativity. At these times I have, very slowly, over the years, learned to wait. In the tiny silences before sleep, or while watching TV I've lost interest in, or even in the aching space after my child's meltdown, I wait for a word or an idea or a character to pop along, say hello, suggest something. Sometimes they don't, and again, very slowly, over the years, I've learned that's OK, too. But when they do, I listen, and scribble down the word or phrase or idea, and there it is: The Magic.

The Magic. It is not easy, but the magic is there all right. Without wishing to sound trite, I think we can prove it is. I think it is a question of trust and of being patient. Will there be a time when something will come along? Yes. There will be times of drought, but I want to reassure you that even the smallest movements can be productive, and you can trust in that. Keep a notebook with you, just in case.

Sara Emmerton

How do I write in the hard days? If I'm sad, I take a notebook and pen out into nature. I bundle up against the cold, go sit on a grass verge and purge on to the page. If I had had an angry, frustrated day? I set my timer for twenty-five minutes and blast hard rock through my headphones. Rage writing can be the most cathartic writing of all.

Rachel Dove

Start on some days with rage. Pour yourself on to the page. Vent. Keep going. Then, later, see what gems there are in there. Perhaps there is only one, and the rest has served its purpose but can now be crossed out as you start to see how a piece of cogent work can be formed – a structured and developed piece of work.

It's about stealing the seconds and daydreaming in brief.

It's about having hundreds of notes on your phone. Ideas half thought.

It's about burning the candle at both ends, and learning when you don't have wick and wax to spare.

It's about loving your craft as much you love those you care for, so that your words bring light in the darkest moments.

Mathew Gallagher

This one is like a poem, or a mantra. I love it, because it's about stealing and things half-done (but still held, in faith) and allowing yourself and your work some love and respect. Because writing, craft, is not trivial. It is not a peripheral thing – it's at the core of who you are. I have been reiterating this, haven't I? Work, done with a lot of distractions, sadness and challenge is still work, and I hope you can evolve enough confidence to know that you can pick up where you left off.

In the swimming pool there are no distractions. I cannot hear the phone or be there for anyone. I lower myself into the warm depths, and once I get into a rhythm, my mind wanders to the world of my current work. The freedom of searching for a word, a sentence, or a phrase on my own terms lies in the muffled bubbles beneath the surface.

Helen O Neill

When I read this, I thought, Do your work where you can and where you need to. Helen writes of this small period of freedom where, for her, ideas are in the water, under the water with her, private and composed. The rhythm might help. There may be a way for you to do this, in exercise, or just alongside your own in-out breaths, carefully observed, as you dwell on a particular idea in a story you want to develop.

After life has intervened, I find restarting writing so hard. My mantra is 'Write rubbish. Tomorrow it will be easier, and better'.

Gill Guest

I say to students and mentees that they must allow themselves to make a mess – to write a Frankendraft, a shit first draft. They can edit as they go, of course, but I blurt the whole thing out, bit by bit, before I touch anything, cross a lot out, kill a few darlings. Your writing will improve; also on some days, it will come more easily than on others. Mistakes really are not so – they're just part of the process. Nothing is wasted.

The voice in my head speaks difficult words, often in the strangest of places. When I write it's as though I'm stealing those thoughts, then I remember they're mine.

Linda Barnes

Only one thing to be said here: claim them, for they ARE yours.

I take a walk in nature. Look as high and as far as I can to the far distance of possibility, allowing my mind to pick up the sense of my feelings and thoughts, transforming them into words that paint pictures for my writing.

Kate Hogan

This is something I do too when I feel lost and particularly sad. I sit with it and then go for a walk. The high and far distance is geographical, a question of scale, but it's not only that. It's also a metaphor, asking yourself how far you can go in your thoughts and feelings and what you will discover. You might go out for a walk. Or you might sit and daydream and ruminate: the terrain is you. Does that make sense?

After dawn prayers, I sit on my velvet mat and write for ten minutes. The pen cannot come away from the page; no distractions – just silence and spirituality.

Sheena Hussain

Just a little period of time, calm time, taken – and note 'the pen cannot come away from the page': that could be discipline, or maybe it's magic, or alchemy – or maybe it's both?

> I find writing down what's in my head like ticking off my to do list – it makes things a little lighter.
>
> Simone Wilby

This is how it is for me too. Work gets done, but it's also a relief, and brings a lightening of pressure. What's in your head might be worries and difficult emotions, but it's also stories. I often look obliquely at my own experience when I am creating a character. Don't forget that you contain a multitude.

> I write to help me feel or to manage whatever is rumbling through my entire body. And some of what I write will be complete and utter rubbish – it might be nonsense, or it might even be playing with words. But it's out there. And then maybe I'll return to it and think, actually this is the framing of the beginnings of something, or, I'll leave it in yet another notebook to stain the page.
>
> Dhruti Shah

I think this could be extended to a much bigger task. For me, my first draft is invariably the book that's in me – that which is 'rumbling through my entire body' and yes, some – nearly all of it – might be rubbish. But as I said in that essay earlier on, Where There's Shit There's Gold,[36] even in scrabbled-together thoughts, there will be gems, or the germ of something. Have trust.

> When I'm really struggling to get started on a piece of writing I get out of the house, but it's not peace and

---

36 Remember the strange little personal essay in chapter one?

quiet I'm after. Cafés, bars, anywhere with background noise – even the garage's office, when my car was being fixed. Going into a different environment where I have no responsibilities forces me to stop procrastinating and get on with it. There's always something that needs doing at home, and it can be hard to ignore, especially when taking time for writing can feel selfish (it's not selfish, by the way, it's essential, but cultural conditioning does not allow for even the bare minimum of self-care).

Rosy Catherine

WELL. That hit a nerve. Conditioning – that's it. Do what Rosy says and, if you possibly can, drop the ball for just a little while, even if you cannot go out. I think we need another permission card.

I am going to write now and no argument about it

I start from where I am, in the midst of the chaos and the tedium, and daydream a little when I can. I use pocket-sized notebooks to try and capture something, however small, from those thoughts. I might mentally explore a phrase I've written (lots of 'what-ifs…' and 'I wonder whys…')

and write some more. Having a few words to reflect back on by the end of the day can remind me I'm working on something, even if I don't quite know what it is yet. I use old-fashioned pen and paper, not an app or anything technology-based, until I've actually got a clear idea of what I want to write. It's cheap, highly portable and uniquely mine. The notebooks are sometimes interesting to look back on – there might be an idea I missed the first time around, but seems more interesting at a later date.

Kathleen Shearer

There is much to reflect on here, but let's start with the first sentence, which goes to the heart of *The Alchemy*: 'I start from where I am, in the midst of the chaos and the tedium...' Work with what you have – right now, if you like. *Always* work with what you have. Also, don't wait for the perfect moment and set-up to start. To me, that's deferring productivity and its ensuing happiness and satisfaction to fate. I also relish this idea of pen and paper (and notebook) being uniquely yours; ours. I believe that reclaiming a little space, sometimes in the form of a physical object and the promise its ownership connotes, are empowering.

Keep a pen and pad by your bed... a way of remembering thoughts wherever you are. When doing the ironing, hoovering, walking the dog or just dropping off to sleep, those times when a chore is dull and no concentration is needed, this is when the mind can drift; this is the space for your imagination to move.

Jane Hall

Spot on. Your brain is a marvellous thing, you know. It will keep on freewheeling, turning and forming ideas, dipping and diving, Isn't that EPIC? I do also see that it feels like an extravagant leap of faith to believe that. But do try. And don't forget the notebook, just in case.

> Never leave yourself a blank page. If you finish a chapter, write one sentence or even one word of the next. Fix it in the edit! Don't worry if it sounds rubbish now, just write – you need a feeling of achievement that finishing a chapter or even a paragraph brings. Just write.
>
> Paul L. Arvidson

This is an interesting suggestion – I like its statement of intent; like a promise to yourself. Also, the feeling of achievement is really important. What can I say? Sometimes there are no solutions to problems; sometimes people are not going to get better: we have to learn to live alongside it and try to carve out just a little space to remind us of who we are and feel that achievement.

> On the hardest days, I remind myself that it is OK to skip a day, but sometimes I need a feeling of accomplishment. In that case, I know that if I'm able to send a text, I'm able to write! I use an app that allows me to write on my phone, tablet and laptop. Even if I write only a sentence or two on my phone while waiting for a bus, then I've achieved my aim for the day!
>
> Félice Le Poer

Yes. Just something, however, whenever, my brave Alchemists.

I find I have most of my good lines first thing in the morning, so I have begun a routine of going to bed very early. Then I wake up early and do some work before anyone else in the house gets up. This can be quite early – it's usually still dark outside. I will have a nice meal of food I prepared the day before and a hot drink. I feel so much better about my writing and my life in general if I can get some writing done before the demands of the day kick in, and it's affirming to myself – sometimes no one else knows I have done that. It's my secret.

Suzanne Iuppa

Aside from the secret, which appeals to the rebel in me, I really love the element of planning and grounding here – can you prepare a little food ahead just for this time, for example? This is one I am going to start using.

For me, writing in tough circumstances is about continuously, gently redefining 'success'. Some days it's making space and time to light a candle, get my laptop out and write until the flow of words slows. But others, it's just tapping out a single sentence on the notes app on my phone or letting my mind wander to my characters as I clean up, or drive, or cook. Sometimes 'writing success' for today is asking for help for tomorrow, or bending a rule (one more treat, one more episode, ten more minutes) so that I can finish a paragraph.

In all of them, the biggest challenge is putting myself first. Making my writing, my well-being, as important as the other demands on me. But as soon as I decide to do that, it almost doesn't matter how much time I get, or how many words I write. Because the decision is what matters, what changes the texture of the day, and what reminds me what it is to feel like me.

Rebecca Lewis-Smith

There is much to comment on here, but I will focus on the adjustment of success: you get to define that, and to redefine it, though I know how hard it can be to slough off societal expectations of a productive life (I am aiming to do that with *The Alchemy*) and of how we achieve success. Then, yes, realise that it's the decision which matters, because it's empowering and an investment in you, and yes: it does change the 'texture' of the day. Finally, bend a rule. Rebellion is healthy.

Adjusting to life after a health change, trauma or accident is a huge challenge. We can't do things the way we used to. But we still want to do things – months in bed is boring – and we can. We can, in fact, work well. It's a matter of learning to work with our body where we are at the moment. Maybe you need more breaks, to work lying down, help to marshal your scattered thoughts into an actionable plan and support to work, even, with the anxiety. By doing the work in front of us, as best we can, in this moment.

Grace Quantock

That's it. What's in front of us, the best we can, this moment. I feel Grace's comments here are a lovely place to end – a killer last line. I'll just add that, from my own perspective, energy-sapping anxiety has been kept at bay by that clear focus. I deal with what is at hand and all else waits. When you are living alongside a set of complex circumstances, there's a lot of what-ifs and catastrophising. It is frightening. 'Marshal your scattered thoughts into an actionable plan' and plant yourself resolutely in the present. Hopefully with a super-fancy notebook.

An Exercise

Read through all of those again and think how you might use these techniques in your own day, your own practice. That is all I am asking you to do. Apart from feeling comforted – because although the rational brain readily tells you that you are not alone if life is difficult, emotions say otherwise. I hope this chapter was of comfort: all the people who have offered suggestions above are writing and aiming to maintain a creative life alongside considerable challenge and demands.

Chapter Eighteen

On Waiting and Thinking

A writing career rarely has a clear trajectory. It can be a stop-start process, where projects go wrong, or entire books might need to be put to one side because they just did not work. Also, writers and agents part company – this happens a lot but is rarely talked about openly; it's quite normal! Sometimes a publisher wants your first book, but not your second, your book does not sell or you receive bad reviews. It is all in the mix. So, as you set out or as you wait to hear about work you have sent out, do rest assured that it is normal to feel nervous, or even frightened, because our writing is important to us, and placing it – or trying to place it – in other hands does make one feel vulnerable. I promise that this feeling subsides a little, but you should never feel ashamed that it exists at all. It is because your work has value; you voice has value: it *matters*.

But while you are waiting, how might you direct your thoughts and look after yourself more? Perhaps you could aim to approach this time with a period of calm reflection, of thought, or have a special journal or notebook which is dedicated to considering how your well-being is doing as you work. Only you can see this, so if you feel cross, frustrated, resentful or overlooked, use it to vent; don't feel embarrassed by these thoughts.

Now, if you have been sending work out to agents or small publishers, stay on top of the administration. Send your queries out in groups of ten to avoid overwhelm and congratulate yourself that you made each one as good as it could be. Keep a note of replies. Rejected? You need to know that rejection is normal and part of the process at all stages – in fact, it is hardwired into creative endeavour. Does this blunt any sense of isolation? Then, do not take it personally, because work is rejected for a myriad of reasons, not all of which are within your control. However, be proactive, so that if you are repeatedly rejected – perhaps over twenty or so times – go back and look at everything again and ask for a pair of eyes you trust to spot what might be wrong. Brooding, feeling resentful and eaten up will stymie your creative process: avoid this. Feel sad, cross, frustrated: this is normal. Then tell yourself sternly to let it go and move on. Use that journal to say things you would not say aloud, if you like, and remember what I have said before about forming a supportive tribe of creatives around you, if you possibly can.[37] Most importantly, do not internalise the tricky stuff. Sit with things and then find a conduit to let 'em out.

When you are querying, it is, of course, fine to stay away from or heavily curate your social-media consumption. It is all too easy to doom-scroll. Yet amazing publishing stories do not readily reveal the fact that everyone's experience and journey in publishing are different – do not show that

---

37 See chapter eleven.

that hot debut was not, after all, an overnight success, but follows many manuscripts still locked in drawers and lots of buns, gin and crying. If you do see success of the kind that you really want, remember to congratulate that person: you never know what's in someone else's heart; it may mean a lot to them; and it feels like, for want of a better phrase, good energy.

Also, there is getting published and staying published. I have found it's helpful to think of playing a very long game here, and to understand that the only thing – THE ONLY THING – you can truly control is the quality of your writing. Only the other day I had work rejected. They thought the writing was 'exquisite'; 'beautiful'. They would have loved to publish it BUT they had work (I could not have known this) about a similar subject in the same time frame; so, even though our treatments and directions were clearly different, from a commercial point of view, it gave pause. There was nothing I could have done. Feel disappointed, then push on, I would say. OR, you could look at publishing yourself, or putting it away and waiting (more waiting!) for a different time and THEN seeing if it no longer gives pause. Work is not wasted, so be cheerful about this.

It would be remiss of me not to mention ghosting here. This is far more challenging than rejections for me. What we mean by 'ghosting' is when you do not hear back from an agent or a publisher you can approach without an agent when a reply is promised or indicated. People are busy, but this is still unacceptable in my view, and having work out there in such a void is upsetting for anyone. I want you to move on; is it possible that you avoided someone who would not be the best person for you, after all? Talk to a friend and share your feelings on this one. It happens at other stages too, and it is very difficult, particularly if you are vulnerable, so do not suffer alone. For both rejection and ghosting, there is no need to brush away healthy feelings, and coping techniques could include sitting with the feelings and letting yourself feel. Understanding that this is a different experience for everyone and that there is no one right way to feel can be a relief, but, gradually, remind yourself gently not to wallow: you do not want to get mired in this, and disappointment is probably more often a point of connection between writers than success!

While you are waiting for replies, what constructive thing can you do – however tiny a step it may be – to develop a career path, hone skills and, importantly, feel both stimulated and settled? I would diversify your reading. Is there a genre or form you have never explored? Go and do that. Do you read books advertised as, say, Book Group Fiction? Then you could try something from a small independent press – perhaps find some literature that is more experimental than you usually ingest. It's exciting, and also reading is part of your creative development and may open doors into new thinking or new ways of writing. You never know! As I said earlier, keep it moving. And I think everything I have described keeps you in the creative zone; keeps it all ticking over.

Now, why not set off on another adventure? Before you do, test that concept on your pulse. Does it feel good to be thinking about new work? Great. Off you go, then – small steps. If, in all honesty, you just feel stressed, I would say it is not worth it – or at least, not just yet. If you do want to press on, here are some ideas, though.

If you have been querying a novel, you may wish to start a new novel, but what about writing in a different form? Try your hand at a short story. Then another. Maybe you will feel enraptured – in which case, why not consider whether you can put together a collection? It is stimulating and may open up new ways, new roads. I mention this because when I was waiting for edits on one book and trying to get an agent, I started writing a short story, having never written one before. That led to a collection – then another. I could not have predicted that. It saved my morale, helped keep me well and led to publication I had not anticipated. I also got my agent with the first short-story collection. Did NOT see that one coming.

In your writing career, it is best to regard your progress as a marathon and not a sprint. Be kind to yourself at all times, and try to relax and be aware of opportunities, because a sensible approach is to regard your writing career as a portfolio.[38] Be bold and pitch an article, offer a poem somewhere, get involved in an event within the writing community – and remember: you may feel small, sometimes vulnerable, but you have as much right to be there as anyone else. Or just express an intent to yourself if that feels too intimidating; take a break, experiment. Whatever you do, as you wait, I shall be rooting for you. And you know, you're not really waiting, after all: you're

---

38 I absolutely believe in this idea for stability, well-being, money, development and longevity. There will be some novelists who may a good wage just from those, but they are very few. Working in this way also helps you to ride the waves of rejection and radio silence. You have more than one project to care about! I've explored it in chapter fourteen.

just between projects. Tell yourself that. I AM THE CAPTAIN OF THIS SHIP! Here's another permission card for you:

I am the captain
of this ship!

Developing autonomy where you can helps stability and good spirits, and much of that autonomy revolves around planning and clear decisions on your part. Now, it may be that your query to an agent or publisher elicits several requests for full manuscripts and subsequent deals, with marvellous phrases such as 'pre-empt', 'hotly contested auction' and possibly a 'swoop' or 'clamour'. (Did I say humour was a vital tool?) It is not likely that this will be the case because, as we have already established, most things fail – but it could happen. I did not expect to marry a man who asked me for directions on a flooded street, but here we are twenty-three years later! You never know. However, dealing with likely outcomes, you may also feel that you have been writing and sending your work into a void, so let me reassure you that this feeling is common and entirely natural. Nonetheless. I suggest that you not start Googling *odds of getting an agent*, or ... *your book published* and, if it feels awful, do not look at recent surveys showing, once more, that being a full-time author is not financially doable unless you are a grandee or have a fabulously wealthy lover supporting you. Actually, DO you have a fabulously wealthy lover? (But I am being nosy – it's really nothing to do with this book.)

Exercises

1. I suggested previously that you might have a special journal or notebook which is dedicated to your observation on how your well-being is doing as you go further. You could also vent your least attractive responses – bile; bitterness… *EWW.* I know: perhaps I ought not to be encouraging this, but there are plenty of dickheads who go on social media and vent, and I know you're *way* more civilised and generous, so into the book and OUT they go. Done. On the other hand, you could just set aside a little regular period of calm reflection to ponder these things, even if you don't write anything down. Consider it *all* as being part of looking after yourself.

2. Bullet-point what you are proud of in the queries that you sent out. It is so important to take time for this, as we frequently move goalposts and fail to note success. Remind yourself that no one publishing route is the same as anyone else's. There are many factors involved which are beyond your control: markets, timing, unexpected events, similar books coming on to agents' desks which you could not possibly have known about. Also, remember that comparison is futile and frequently depressing: be the captain of your own ship and be proud of yourself.

3. It's important to reclaim a little power. So, for example, if you have queried an agent and there is no reply (when one is promised on their website), chase once and give them (do not tell them) a deadline to respond. If you keep a spreadsheet, write 'rejected' – by YOU. May I add that a sense of humour is an excellent addition to your armoury and that you are not the last turkey in the shop, dear writer?

4. Think about times where you have felt safe and looked after; when you have felt you could express yourself freely. Think about people with whom you felt this. That feeling is what you are aiming for with the little community you build, slowly but surely.

5. Every week – or less frequently if you feel overloaded – make a note (typed or in writing) of things that made you feel good in your writing or interactions with the writing and publishing community. Now find ways to get more of that.

Chapter Nineteen

A Series of Prompts

Things to make you go OOOH!

The point of this chapter is to shake you down a little bit and prompt you to think, re-think and notice things. You do NOT have to agree with all − or any − of it, but please do consider my ideas here.

In Walt Whitman's 'Song of Myself', from his *Leaves of Grass* (1867), he says this:

*You shall no longer take things at second or third hand, nor look
    through the eyes of the dead, nor feed on the spectres in books;
You shall not look through my eyes either, nor take things from me:
You shall listen to all sides, and filter them from yourself.*

So I want to encourage you to do just this. I have, throughout this book, said that I wanted you, always, to work with what you have; now I want to add that you should not be frightened of not having a degree or MA in Creative Writing, as many have and as many think must be a prerequisite. There are many reasons for doing such a course, and I do teach on them sometimes, but still I would counsel that they are one possibility only. So, think on what you have, work with what you have. You may have little or no formal education. Well, now, I have been involved in education for decades; I also have a big family. Let me say that being highly educated is not the same as being intelligent; that being book-smart or able to pass exams may be allied with very high intelligence – genius, even – but clearly it is not necessarily the case. Let's be radical, then: you contain a multitude: what do you already have? Isn't it possible that you have many brilliant things fermenting in your mind? I think the key here is kicking back from societal expectations and adopting a position of trust in your intellectual capacity, imagination and your own eyes and ears. You are full of knowledge, thought and imagination, and the way in which you see the world will be subtly (or less so) unique to you, so push more into the world and see what you can find out. Exciting, isn't it?

Now, do you only react to bad things? Ever thought about that? What a simple concept!

You react to them because bad things often require you to take action; to deal with things. Yet look at the good things we fail to notice – about the world and about ourselves. Make a pact with yourself that you will always regard the good things you have done and, regarding your writing, that you will notice your productivity and say good things to yourself about that. Otherwise take it from one who knows: if you keep moving the goalposts, you'll never take delight in the work you have already produced, according to your own light.

Here is a startling but really quite obvious thought. Once you did not have language. Just think of the words you have yet to find and experience. Words are glorious, subtle things. Think too about which things, which concepts and experiences, can be shaped by having *more words*. This is an argument for reading, overhearing and listening in; for acquiring a richer vocabulary.

What about taking a chance on different writing? It is entirely possible that work has stalled because you're writing in a way which is, at present, inimical to you. It may be that a different style or genre would suit you more. Even a different form – at least for a while. Experiment.

There was a time when your father was a fish. Later on, an ape. You have a lot of relatives. Why am I mentioning this? Because it is extraordinary. It is extraordinary that we have this planet, with everything coming together. Think of this to make you go *OOOH*. At one point there were trillions of atoms doing their atomic dance, moving in and out of form, and they had to meet up and get on well and coalesce to form you, and you are unique and will never exist again. Yes, one day atoms will quietly disassemble when time's up, but even so. The thing that blows my mind is that atoms do this epic thing, but they are not even alive – they are particles without mind and consciousness, and yet they made you and will keep you alive. The elements that make you were born in the stars. It is all miraculous. So do not waste it. Don't stay mired in self-doubt, just start, in however tiny a way.

Also, keep your sense of wonder. There it is, behind human idiocy and rhetoric and cant, something gorgeous: remember to wonder at it, and take that and run with it. Create. It works for me, but it does require you to remind yourself of what is astonishing. Another thing: you already are astonishing. Burnish it a little.

There are people who are in love with you, and you will never know it. Round the corner may be a person who will change your life in a good way, and there will be lives you have changed and yet you never even knew it. Another set of sensational things. Be alive to the possibility of radical and good change and know, with your writing, that just because something has always been a certain way does not mean it will always be like this. It went wrong before? You stalled? Oh, braveheart, off you go again, because you never know and won't know until you leave yourself open to possibility.

It is possible you try ambition, and it works.

It's possible you have yet to hear the music that will bring you to your knees.

The love of your life may round the corner. See that not-very-interesting corner by the pavement with the chipped edge? Yeah. That corner.

Keep the fire in your eyes, retrieve and retain your sense of wonder, dare to experiment, discover and play with new words, and please believe that what you have to say is important and we need your words in the world. Now does this make you go OOOH? It does me, because I'm looking forward to seeing what you might create. And, in the spirit of this book, regardless of the context in which you create it and however slow and halting the progress was.

Anna

Rather than a formal exercise I'd like to suggest this: go and sit somewhere comfortable; really pamper yourself, if you can. Then dare to do something. I'd like you to note down what you really want to see in your writing. You might sit and write longhand, or lie in bed and do this as voice notes. Even if it seems ridiculously ambitious or daft, or you feel that no one else will understand. It is good to clarify this.

There is a second strand. If you feel up to it – that is, if this does not make you feel too tender – you might also note *why* you want these things. Why? To check in with yourself honestly: do you really want them, or do you feel you just ought to, or are you proving a point? There must be honesty here – and joy. I hope that makes sense.

Chapter Twenty

A Conclusion

A final thought. I said that this book is for everyone, but it is clear I have a particular eye on those who meet significant challenges. Those groups – experiencing difficulty – have also helped me enormously in adjusting to fatigue and pain and the demands that helping one of my sons to heal has had on me over a long period. So, there is something else which we need to say, and it is about providing definitions for yourself.

Who are you?

Here is who I am. I am not always very well, and I have a great deal of doubt about my ability and nervousness with managing industry. It was impressed on me, growing up, in secondary school and by my immediate family, that I was somewhat of a waste of space, and the combined effort did me permanent damage. There are additional needs within my immediate family, and we have been radically let down by multiple agencies. It is really painful, and I manage it alongside health challenges, aiming to work and write books. I have already told you a lot about myself, my life: I reiterate it here because it is vital you understand that my books have been made in this context and, until recently, with very little support. Then, it took me decades to start writing – to *start*. Not to get published; to start. Once I got involved in publishing, I met some lovely people, but had some tricky experiences with a small handful of industry professionals. I find as much positive input as I need from whatever sources I can specifically so that I can fulfil my personal goals in a way that makes sense to me, as a complete, rounded human being. This is, however, a daily job: to focus on what I think and not allow myself to be a composite of others' opinions. None of this was a smooth road – but does it matter? I am still here, after all!

I'll tell you what, though. If I *hadn't* had these experiences, and if I weren't managing the challenges I have (please bear in mind that I cannot elucidate on the nature of everything here, because these are others' stories and I will not intrude on anyone else's agency), then I would not be here sharing *The Alchemy* with you.

Look at our lives. Even when the outside world says that something is limited, or appears to say that, I think we know, don't we really, that they are rich, varied and interesting? Those things rest on the power and texture of your thought and your engagement – and that engagement need only be thinking and noticing.

Yes, rich, interesting, and varied. Pulsing with life.

And, as Josie George says in *A Still Life*, we really don't get anywhere on our own.[39] Writing is largely a solitary craft, but everything around it is not. So please do not be afraid to ask questions or talk to your tribe.

---

39 Josie George, *A Still Life* (London: Bloomsbury Publishing, 2021), p. 191.

I hope that in working towards a book, a sustained piece of writing, in small and gentle steps, you have not felt alone, or that you have felt less alone. I hope that you have felt *The Alchemy* alongside you as a guide to work and as a friend. That was my intention.

Anna

Kit, Tips and Prompts

Use any or all of these, or chuck the lot if it does not work for you. What supports you and how do you keep at it when things get tough?

1. Having Other Work on the go, whatever it might be.
2. Going for long walks.
3. Accepting I am just a person and I do not have superpowers.
4. Try not to allow yourself to get distracted by social media or those around you. Take a hot drink, gather your characters around you and start the conversation. Even if it's short!
5. Clear your laptop of tabs on the night before (anticipated) writing days or time so that your novel is the only thing you see when you set to work. I say this as someone who frequently has huge numbers of tabs open. Take the time: consider it work admin.
6. Leave your phone in another room.
7. Write even just a few words of what you plan to do next because, that way, you always have a start. This is a small morale boost for you. And small things, as we have established, add up.

8. You might want silence, so try earplugs or noise-cancelling headphones and ambient music – maybe lyric-free. Is this a possibility? Alternatively, if you find it helps to have white noise, which some do, pick up a little desk fan for a fiver.

9. Why not try jotting down a brief outline of the next scene you need to write? That way, when you next go back – do this the night before if you anticipate some writing time ahead – you're not going in cold to new work. You could make yourself a daily voice note. Again, this can be a lovely little morale boost because it feels like you have already made a start.

10. This *writing-a-book* thing can be intimidating, so try to put aside the idea of publication or thoughts that one day this book will have/might have an audience. Why not try dictating a few things to your phone, write something just to amuse yourself, try free writing? Experiment and play. For example, you might have something you want to explore, but consider doing it via another form – such as a recipe? A shopping list? Chuck in some drawings, even if you are terrible at art! Play around. I think doing so can help you relax and make you feel less self-conscious.

Kit

Aside from whatever you tap on, here is my writing kit:

- Roget's Thesaurus on the desk, or kitchen table, or wherever.
- Two mugs of coloured pens and pencils. I don't necessarily use them all; I just find the colour gives me a boost.
- For your desk – or whatever your writing area is: flowers. AHA. Can you stretch to an 80p bunch of fake peonies from Home Bargains? I add whatever little bits of evergreen I can find, and people go, OOH LOOK AT THOSE LOVELY FLOWERS, and I go, OOH JUST AN ADMIRER. YES YES, THEY LEFT ME FLOWERS.
- Coloured post-its. It helps me to mark where I left off if I've printed work off and am proofing and editing. It's just a little prompt which is helpful when I am particularly tired.
- Oils: lavender, patchouli and geranium. I swear by a small pot of tiger balm to sniff, and I also have a little spray bottle I keep in the fridge overnight and bring to the desk with me – just water and a couple of drops of lavender oil – and I mist my face with it. That grounds and comforts me, and if I am writing about difficult things, or difficult thoughts come bubbling up, I find it helps me sit with that and deal better with it. This is a practice I've been doing for decades. My husband bought me a spray called Total De-Stress and, of course, it's showing off a bit because it doesn't destress totally – but it's a mix of geranium, orange and nutmeg. After

it's empty, I fill it with water and it still smells good for months and months.

- A little cushion for your chair, just for this purpose? Mine is a small one and it says 'Queen Bee', and the bee on it looks particularly jaunty, so it does the trick.
- A blanket: my emotions are labile and, as I write this, there is a lot going on around me, some of it is extremely sad and it's all bound up with being let down for years by resources and professionals and others whose remit it was to help and who did the opposite... And oh, I can get overcome by those thoughts as I'm tapping away or reading at my desk. It's at this point that I relish my weighted blanket on my legs, which acts like a hug. I swear by it. It's medium-weight; if you're hardcore, go heavy. The weighted blanket got this book written.
- A hot drink. I KNOW it seems trivial, but these acts of self-care have a big impact. Yorkshire tea, decent coffee – I rather like hot water and lemon, and once a day I make myself a really nice hot chocolate, made with milk.
- A hot-water bottle: those long ones are good. You could have a bunny cover. However you do it, try hot in winter and cool in summer. I love it. I've had a bottle every day since my teens.

Write your own list here? Yep: scribble in this book. Doodle too.

Acknowledgements and Thank-Yous

For Ned, Elijah, Isaac and Caleb, to my pals and the sturdy group I met online who are SEND parents, for my community and for the chronic illness and disability communities. To John Mitchinson and Rina Gill, who took an early interest in this book. To Joanne Harris, who is such a support to so many and makes publishing feel better. To Dr Jonathan Taylor, Associate Professor of Creative Writing, University of Leicester, Dr Shelley Harris, Director of Creative Writing, University of Reading, and Kat Ashton, Director of Courses at Jericho Writers: they all read and supported the book, and to know them is a joy. To Professors Rob Edgar and Abi Curtis at York St John, whose encouragement towards the PhD fed into confidence everywhere, and so into *The Alchemy*, and also to the wonderful Abbie Headon, whose support at a crucial moment led to so much: I shall never forget that. To Dr Chris Laoutaris, Associate Professor Shakespeare Institute, University of Birmingham, for writing such a moving foreword to the book. And, above all here, to my friend and publisher, Will Dady, who made this book happen and thought it was important – just as he has with two other books this year!

Thank you to those of you who allowed me to include their thoughts in this book by quotation. The inaugural Curae Prize, for writer-carers, has made this, even so, a red-letter year so huge congratulations to our two winners, Kate Blincoe and Helen O Neill. Kisses to Jericho Writers, who have been so lovely to work with during this period, and my brilliant gang of mentees, who are such a joy: Brie, Ida, Luisa, Danni, Molly, Claire and Sarah, then Kate, Ed, Tom, Bshash, Alison, Claire F. and Claire G., Jen: I have been so lucky. To Alexi, Corrina, the Susies, Sue, Julie, Sarah, Louise, Mari, Lucy, Em, Ellie, Jane, Rose, Sue, Barbara and Peter – and to my aunts, uncles and cousins, and to our community where we live. Love you.

Finally, a special mention to a lovely friend, Angela Vick, whom we lost just as I finished the book. She had been a parent of young people I taught, then a colleague and pal – and she always championed my work and comforted and supported me, and she was a goddess.

And a special thank you to readers of everything I make: it's because of you that just after this book is published, I am back at university

…And once more, in particular, thanks to my beautiful eldest boy, Elijah. This book is for you and yes, I know I am deeply embarrassing.

Anna

The Alchemy Forum

The Alchemy is about writing a book – a work of fiction of whatever kind – when you thought you could not. It is a book for everyone, but with a particular eye on those who are tired and lacking in confidence; those who are disabled, chronically ill or perhaps care for a loved one who would struggle without them. Essentially, this has been me for some time now, and that is how I know about productivity – and how I know about challenging what it is; how we think of and understand productivity in terms of a creative project.

Alongside the book, we have created a forum for you, to supplement the pages of *The Alchemy*, and here you will find downloadable resources, and there is space for sharing your news, responses and progress, because the Alchemy is a community.

RESOURCES • NEWS • COLUMN
RESPONSES & THOUGHTS

RENARDPRESS.COM/THE-ALCHEMY

ABOUT THE AUTHOR

ANNA VAUGHT is an English teacher, Creative Writing teacher, mentor, editor and author of several books, including *Saving Lucia*, *Famished*, *Ravished*, *The Zebra and Lord Jones*, *These Envoys of Beauty* and the forthcoming essay collection, *To Melt the Stars*. Her short creative works and features have been widely published, and she has written for the national press and has had a column with *The Bookseller* and *Mslexia*. In 2022 Anna launched The Curae, a new literary prize for carers. Anna is also a guest university lecturer, a tutor for Jericho Writers, and volunteers with young people from disadvantaged backgrounds. She is currently a PhD by Published Works student at York St John University, where she is writing on magical realism and trauma. She is the mother of three sons, comes from a large Welsh family and lives in Wiltshire.

ANNAVAUGHTWRITES.COM 🌐 🐦 @BOOKWORMVAUGHT